HICKENMUSSELSBAS
RNUTSQUASHSALMON
CCH MSRED
RME ANNELLONI
COTTAOLIVEOILLPR
RELLAPASTAGARLIC
SPENNESAUSAGESPE
RFALLEBOLOGNESEB
TPEPPERHAMCOURG
ERSHALLOTBECHAME
RYHADDOCKDILLMAS
BSLEM AMICOD
OMATO ARROT

Annabel Karmel
Top 100 Pasta Dishes

100 easy, everyday recipes for the whole family

EBURY
PRESS

To my children, Nicholas, Lara and Scarlett

10 9 8 7 6 5 4 3 2 1

Published in 2010 by Ebury Press, an imprint of Ebury Publishing
A Random House Group Company

The Random House Group Limited Reg. No. 954009

Addresses for companies within the Random House Group can be found at
www.randomhouse.co.uk

A CIP catalogue record for this book is available from the British Library

The Random House Group Limited supports the Forest Stewardship Council (FSC),
the leading international forest certification organisation. All our titles that are printed
on Greenpeace-approved FSC certified paper carry the FSC logo. Our paper procurement
policy can be found at www.rbooks.co.uk/environment

To buy books by your favourite authors and register for offers visit www.rbooks.co.uk

Printed and bound in China by C & C Offset Printing Co., Ltd.

Design & illustrations: Smith & Gilmour Ltd, London
Photography: Dave King
Food stylist: Seiko Hatfield
Props stylist: Jo Harris
Copy editor: Helena Caldon

ISBN 9780091937720

- ⚆ SUITABLE FROM 7 MONTHS
- ⚇ MAKES 4 PORTIONS
- 🕐 PREPARATION TIME: 5 MINUTES / COOKING TIME: 20 MINUTES
- ❄ SUITABLE FOR FREEZING

Pasta with tomato and mascarpone sauce

Five different vegetables are blended into this tasty tomato sauce. Passata is simply sieved tomatoes, and you can buy it in any supermarket. Mascarpone is good for babies as they need proportionately more fat in their diets than adults due to their rapid growth rate. If you don't have any, use double cream or cream cheese instead.

1 tbsp olive oil
1 red onion, peeled and chopped
30 g (1 oz) carrot, diced
30 g (1 oz) courgette, diced
15 g (½ oz) celery, diced
1 garlic clove, crushed
50 g (2 oz) button mushrooms, chopped
400 ml (14 fl oz) passata or 1 x 400 g can chopped tomatoes
2 tbsp apple juice
60 g (2½ oz) pasta shells
2 tbsp torn basil leaves (optional)
3 tbsp mascarpone
3 tbsp grated Parmesan

★ Heat the oil in a saucepan and sauté the onion, carrot, courgette and celery for 5 minutes. Add the garlic and sauté for 1 minute. Add the button mushrooms and sauté for 2 minutes. Stir in the passata or chopped tomatoes with the apple juice and simmer for 10 minutes with the lid on, stirring occasionally.

★ Meanwhile, cook the pasta shells according to the instructions on the packet. Drain.

★ Remove the tomato sauce from the heat, add the basil (if using) and blend in a food processor. Return to the pan and stir in the mascarpone and Parmesan. Stir the sauce into the drained pasta.

VARIATION: To make a creamy tomato chicken Bolognese sauce, simply add 75 g (3 oz) diced cooked chicken breast at the same time as the mushrooms.

Tomato, sweet potato and cheese sauce with pasta shells

This delicious tomato sauce is enriched with vegetables. It is very versatile; you can mix it with pasta, as here, or blend it together with fish or chicken.

1 tbsp olive oil

1 onion, chopped

1 garlic clove, chopped

225 g (8 oz) sweet potato, peeled and chopped

2 medium carrots, peeled and sliced (approx. 125 g/4½ oz)

1 x 400 g (14 oz) can chopped tomatoes

200 ml (7 fl oz) vegetable stock or water

100 g (3½ oz) organic baby shell pasta

60 g (2½ oz) Cheddar cheese, grated

★ Heat the oil in a saucepan and sauté the onion for about 4 minutes until softened. Add the garlic and sauté for 1 more minute. Stir in the sweet potato and carrots, then stir in the tomatoes and vegetable stock or water. Bring to the boil, stirring, then cover the pan and simmer for about 30 minutes until the vegetables are tender.

★ Meanwhile, cook the pasta according to the instructions on the packet. Drain.

★ Once cooked, allow the sauce to cool slightly, then blend the sauce to a purée and stir in the cheese until melted. Mix the drained pasta with the sauce.

Baby 9

SUITABLE FROM 7 MONTHS

MAKES 4 PORTIONS

PREPARATION TIME: 8 MINUTES / COOKING TIME: 20 MINUTES

SUITABLE FOR FREEZING

Pasta stars with carrot and tomato

Stir these tiny organic pasta stars into your baby's favourite purée for a gradual introduction to more lumpy food. Interestingly, carrots are more nutritious when cooked with a little butter or oil, as the betacarotene they contain is absorbed more readily. The same is true of tomatoes; they are rich in lycopene, a powerful antioxidant which is better absorbed by our bodies when tomatoes are cooked in a little oil or butter.

2 medium carrots (approx. 125 g/
4½ oz), peeled and sliced
20 g (¾ oz) butter
3 medium tomatoes (about 225 g/
8 oz), skinned, seeded and
quartered
40 g (1½ oz) grated Cheddar cheese
2 fresh basil leaves, torn into pieces
40 g (1½ oz) Make It Easy gluten-
free mini pasta stars

★ Steam the carrots for about 20 minutes or until tender. Heat the butter in a separate pan then add the tomatoes and sauté until mushy. Remove from the heat and stir in the cheese until melted, then add the fresh basil.

★ Meanwhile, cook the mini pasta stars in boiling water according to the instructions on the packet. Drain.

★ Purée the cooked carrots together with 3 tablespoons of the liquid from the bottom of the steamer using an electric hand blender. Blend together with the tomato and cheese mixture and stir in the drained pasta stars.

Pasta shells with salmon and broccoli

Fish is good for the brain; omega-3 essential fatty acids are found in oily fish and make up 40 per cent of the brain. A baby's brain grows rapidly between birth and three years, and most of this growth takes place in the first year, so it's important to introduce fish such as salmon early on. Fish is quick and easy to prepare and delicious combined with root vegetables.

50 g (2 oz) salmon fillet
150 ml (¼ pint) unsalted vegetable or chicken stock
40 g (1½ oz) baby pasta shells
a knob of butter
½ small onion, finely chopped
2 tsp plain flour
100 ml (3½ fl oz) milk
50 g (2 oz) broccoli, roughly chopped
3 tbsp crème fraîche
3 tbsp Parmesan cheese, grated
1 tsp lemon juice
½ tsp fresh dill, chopped
½ tsp fresh chives, chopped

★ To cook the salmon, either poach the fish in a little of the stock over a low heat for 3–4 minutes, or until it flakes easily with a fork, or cook in a microwave with a couple of tablespoons of stock for about 2 minutes.

★ Meanwhile, cook the pasta according to the packet instructions. Drain.

★ To make the sauce, melt the butter in a saucepan. Add the onion and sauté for 3–4 minutes until just soft. Add the flour and mix together, then blend in the remaining stock and milk. Bring to the boil. Add the broccoli and simmer, covered, for 5–6 minutes until soft.

★ Whiz in a food processor until smooth. Stir in the crème fraîche, Parmesan, lemon juice, herbs and cooked salmon. Simmer for 2 minutes. Serve the drained pasta with the sauce.

BABY

Contents

SUITABLE FROM 8 MONTHS

MAKES 4 PORTIONS

PREPARATION TIME: 8 MINUTES /
COOKING TIME: 15 MINUTES

SUITABLE FOR FREEZING

SUITABLE FROM 9 MONTHS

MAKES 4 PORTIONS

PREPARATION TIME: 8 MINUTES /
COOKING TIME: 18 MINUTES

SUITABLE FOR FREEZING

Mushroom and spinach pasta

60 g (2½ oz) baby pasta shells
10 g (½ oz) butter
50 g (2 oz) onion, finely diced
50 g (2 oz) chestnut mushrooms,
   finely diced
1 garlic clove, crushed
10 g (½ oz) plain flour
250 ml (9 fl oz) milk
¼ tsp fresh thyme, chopped
30 g (1 oz) Parmesan, grated
30 g (1 oz) baby spinach, finely chopped

★ Cook the pasta according to the instructions on the packet. Drain.
★ Melt the butter in a saucepan, add the onion, cover with a lid and sauté for 8 minutes or until softened. Add the mushrooms and fry for 3 minutes. Add the garlic and fry for 2 minutes. Add the flour, then add the milk, stirring until thickened. Add the thyme, Parmesan and spinach and stir until wilted.
★ Stir in the drained pasta.

Chicken and sweetcorn pasta

60 g (2½ oz) baby pasta shells
15 g (½ oz) butter
50 g (2 oz) onion, finely diced
75 g (3 oz) chicken breast, chopped
   into small pieces
30 g (1 oz) canned or frozen sweetcorn
15 g (½ oz) plain flour
250 ml (9 fl oz) milk
½ tsp Dijon mustard
25 g (1 oz) Parmesan cheese, grated
1 tsp chives, finely chopped

★ Cook the pasta according to the instructions on the packet. Drain.
★ To make the sauce, melt the butter in a saucepan, then add the onion, cover with a lid and sauté for about 8 minutes until soft. Add the chicken and sauté for 2 minutes. Add the flour, stir over the heat for 1 minute, then add the milk, stirring until thickened. Add the sweetcorn and mustard and simmer for 5 minutes, then remove from the heat and add the Parmesan and chives.
★ Stir in the drained pasta.

 SUITABLE FROM 9 MONTHS

MAKES 3 PORTIONS

PREPARATION TIME: 10 MINUTES / COOKING TIME: 25 MINUTES

SUITABLE FOR FREEZING

Hidden vegetable bolognese

This Bolognese is good with pasta shapes or you could mix it with some potato mashed with a little butter and milk and maybe just a little grated Cheddar instead of salt. You could also make this with minced turkey or chicken.

1 tbsp light olive oil
2 shallots, chopped (approx. 50 g/2 oz)
50 g (2 oz) diced carrot
20 g (¾ oz) diced celery
1 small garlic clove, crushed
50 g (2 oz) peeled butternut squash, chopped
1 x 200 g (7 oz) can chopped tomatoes or ½ x 400 g (14 oz) can
150 g (5½ oz) lean minced beef
1 tsp tomato purée
100 ml (3½ fl oz) unsalted beef or chicken stock, or water
1 tsp fresh thyme leaves
50 g (2 oz) organic baby star pasta

★ Heat the oil in a saucepan and sauté the shallots, carrot and celery over a low heat for 7–8 minutes until softened. Add the garlic and cook for 30 seconds. Add the butternut squash, pour over the chopped tomatoes and cook for 5 minutes.

★ Meanwhile, brown the minced meat in a frying pan with no oil. Transfer the vegetables to a food processor and blend until smooth. Put the blended vegetables back in the pan, add the tomato purée, stock, thyme and the browned mince. Cover and cook for 12–15 minutes, adding a little more stock if necessary.

★ Meanwhile, cook the pasta stars according to the instructions on the packet. Once cooked, drain and toss with the sauce.

Tomato sauce with butternut squash and red lentils

This tasty sauce is enriched with lentils and butternut squash. Lentils are a good cheap source of protein and iron, and as such are important in a vegetarian diet. Butternut squash is rich in betacarotene, which is important for growth, healthy skin and good vision. With non-meat sources of iron such as lentils, wholegrain cereals or green leafy vegetables you need to give vitamin C at the same meal to help the absorption of iron.

1 tbsp sunflower oil
50 g (2 oz) chopped onion
50 g (2 oz) chopped carrot
15 g (½ oz) celery, chopped
30 g (1 oz) split red lentils
110 g (4 oz) butternut squash
200 ml (7 fl oz) passata (or use canned chopped tomatoes)
150 ml (5 fl oz) water
50 g (2 oz) baby pasta shells
40 g (1½ oz) mature Cheddar cheese, grated

★ Heat the oil and sauté the onion, carrot and celery for 5 minutes.
★ Rinse the lentils and add to the pan. Add the butternut squash and cook, stirring, for 1 minute. Pour in the passata or chopped tomatoes and water. Cover and cook over a low heat for about 30 minutes.
★ Meanwhile, cook the pasta according to the instructions on the packet. Drain.
★ Remove the squash and lentils mixture from the heat and stir in the cheese until melted. Purée in a blender, then stir in the drained pasta.

☻ SUITABLE FROM 8 MONTHS

🍲 MAKES 4 PORTIONS

🕐 PREPARATION TIME: 10 MINUTES /
COOKING TIME: 18 MINUTES

❄ SUITABLE FOR FREEZING

☻ SUITABLE FROM 7 MONTHS

🍲 MAKES 2 PORTIONS

🕐 PREPARATION TIME: 5 MINUTES /
COOKING TIME: 9 MINUTES

❄ NOT SUITABLE FOR FREEZING

Baby vegetable pasta

As your baby gets older it is important to encourage him to chew, so dice vegetables instead of pureeing them. Frozen peas and sweetcorn are good standbys to keep in your freezer.

50 g (2 oz) baby shell pasta
10 g (½ oz) butter
50 g (2 oz) onion, finely chopped
30 g (1 oz) carrot, finely diced
30 g (1 oz) red pepper, finely diced
30 g (1 oz) frozen sweetcorn
30 g (1 oz) frozen peas
10 g (½ oz) plain flour
250 ml (9 fl oz) vegetable stock
2 tbsp basil, chopped
1 tsp lemon juice
30 g (1 oz) Parmesan cheese, grated

★ Cook the pasta according to the instructions on the packet. Drain.

★ Melt the butter in a saucepan. Add the onion, carrot and pepper, cover with a lid and sauté for 10 minutes until nearly soft. Add the sweetcorn and peas and sauté for 2 minutes. Add the flour, then add the stock, stirring until thickened. Simmer for 3 minutes, then add the basil, lemon juice and Parmesan.

★ Stir in the drained pasta.

Confetti pasta

50g (2 oz) orzo or other
small pasta shapes
30g (1½ oz) carrot, diced
30g (1½ oz) frozen peas
1½ tbsp cream
3 tbsp Parmesan, grated

★ Cook the pasta for 6 minutes together with the diced carrot. Add the peas for the last 2–3 minutes, then drain.

★ Stir the cream and Parmesan into the pasta and serve.

SUITABLE FROM 8 MONTHS

MAKES 3 PORTIONS

PREPARATION TIME: 8 MINUTES PLUS 20 MINUTES FOR INFUSING / COOKING TIME: 18 MINUTES

NOT SUITABLE FOR FREEZING

Cheese sauce with butternut squash

If you have time it's nice to infuse the milk to give it extra flavour, but you can skip this step if you prefer. For older babies I blend half the sauce with the butternut squash and leave the other half diced so it has some texture.

400 ml (14 fl oz) milk
40 g (1½ oz) onions, cut into wedges
1 bay leaf
3 parsley stalks
3 peppercorns
10 g (½ oz) butter
75 g (3 oz) carrot, diced
50 g (2 oz) squash, diced
10 g (½ oz) flour
60 g (2½ oz) baby pasta shells
¾ tsp Dijon mustard
20 g (¾ oz) Parmesan, grated
20 g (¾ oz) mature Cheddar, grated

★ First, infuse the milk. Put the milk, onion wedges, bay leaf, parsley stalks and peppercorns into a pan. Bring to the boil and simmer gently for 20–30 minutes, then strain through a sieve into a jug.
★ Melt the butter in a clean saucepan. Add the carrot and squash and sauté for 5 minutes. Add the flour, then the strained milk, stirring until thickened. Simmer for 10 minutes until the ingredients are soft.
★ Meanwhile, cook the pasta according to the instructions on the packet. Drain.
★ Whiz the vegetables and sauce in a food processor until smooth. For older babies, whiz half the vegetables and leave the other half diced. Add the mustard and cheeses. Stir in the drained pasta.

SUITABLE FROM 7 MONTHS

MAKES 3 PORTIONS

PREPARATION TIME: 10 MINUTES /
COOKING TIME: 25 MINUTES

SUITABLE FOR FREEZING

SUITABLE FROM 9 MONTHS

MAKES 4 PORTIONS

PREPARATION TIME: 8 MINUTES/
COOKING TIME: 15 MINUTES

SUITABLE FOR FREEZING

Little stars with minced beef

60 g (2½ oz) pasta stars
10 g (½ oz) butter
30 g (1 oz) onion, finely diced
50 g (2 oz) carrot, finely diced
30 g (1 oz) celery, finely diced
75 g (3 oz) minced beef
½ tsp redcurrant jelly
10 g (½ oz) plain flour
250 ml (9 fl oz) beef stock
1 tsp tomato purée
1 tsp Worcestershire sauce
½ tsp fresh thyme

★ Cook the pasta according to the instructions on the packet. Drain.
★ Melt the butter in a saucepan and add the onion, carrot and celery and sauté for 5 minutes. Add the mince to the vegetables and brown for 5 minutes, breaking up the lumps with a fork as you stir. Add the redcurrant jelly and sauté for 1 minute. Add the flour, then the stock, tomato purée, Worcestershire sauce and thyme. Simmer for 10 minutes, uncovered.
★ Stir in the drained pasta.

Cauliflower, broccoli and pea pasta

60 g (2½ oz) baby shell pasta
10 g (½ oz) butter
50 g (2 oz) onion, finely chopped
50 g (2 oz) tiny cauliflower florets
50 g (2 oz) tiny broccoli florets
30 g (1 oz) frozen peas
10 g (½ oz) plain flour
250 ml (9 fl oz) milk
30 g (1 oz) Parmesan, grated
½ tsp Dijon mustard

★ Cook the pasta according to the instructions on the packet. Drain.
★ Melt the butter in a pan, add the onion and sauté for 5 minutes. Then add the cauliflower, broccoli and peas. Sauté for 5 minutes, then add the flour and milk, stirring until thickened. Simmer for a few minutes, then spoon half of the mixture into a bowl.
★ Whiz the remaining mixture in the pan using a hand blender until smooth. Stir in the Parmesan and mustard, then return the reserved unblended mixture to the pan with the drained pasta.

SUITABLE FROM 9 MONTHS

MAKES 4 PORTIONS

PREPARATION TIME: 8 MINUTES / COOKING TIME: 20 MINUTES

SUITABLE FOR FREEZING

Fruity chicken curry with pasta

Korma paste has a slightly sweet flavour which is ideal for younger palates. Dried apricots are rich in betacarotene and also contain iron. I prefer to use organic dried apricots which are brown in colour; commercial ones are often treated with sulphur dioxide (E220) to preserve their bright orange colour, which can trigger an asthma attack in susceptible babies.

60 g (2½ oz) baby pasta shells
2 tsp sunflower oil
50 g (2 oz) onion, finely diced
¼ tsp fresh ginger, grated
2 tsp mild korma curry paste
150 ml (¼ pint) chicken stock
100 ml (3½ fl oz) coconut milk
15 g (½ oz) dried apricots, roughly
    chopped
50 g (2 oz) butternut squash,
    finely diced
75 g (3 oz) chicken breast,
    chopped into small pieces

★ Cook the pasta according to the instructions on the packet. Drain.
★ Heat the oil in a saucepan. Add the onion and ginger and sauté for 5 minutes. Add the curry paste, then the stock and coconut milk. Add the apricots and squash. Bring to the boil, then simmer, covered, for 10 minutes until the squash is tender. Whiz until smooth using a hand blender.
★ Fry the chicken for 3–4 minutes, then add the sauce. Finally, stir in the drained pasta.

☺ SUITABLE FROM 8 MONTHS

MAKES 3 PORTIONS

PREPARATION TIME: 8 MINUTES / COOKING TIME: 25 MINUTES

❋ SUITABLE FOR FREEZING

Tomato and Mediterranean vegetable sauce

Adding diced apple and apple juice gives a sweetness to this sauce that appeals to babies. If you don't have any aubergine, use diced carrot or butternut squash instead, but you will need to add this together with the onion so that it cooks long enough to soften.

50 g (2 oz) baby pasta shells
2 tsp oil
75 g (3 oz) onion, finely chopped
1 small garlic clove, crushed
15 g (½ oz) red pepper, finely diced
15 g (½ oz) aubergine, finely diced
15 g (½ oz) apple, peeled and
    finely diced
15 g (½ oz) celery, finely diced
30 g (1 oz) courgette, finely diced
100 ml (3½ fl oz) apple juice (I used
    Copella cloudy apple juice)
300 g (10½ oz) chopped tomatoes
1 tsp sundried tomato paste
1 tbsp basil

★ Cook the pasta according to the instructions on the packet. Drain.
★ Heat the oil in a saucepan, add the onion and sauté for 5 minutes. Add the garlic and cook for 1 minute, then add the remaining vegetables and apple and sauté for 5 minutes. Next, add the apple juice, tomatoes and sundried tomato paste. Bring to the boil then simmer, covered, for 10 minutes.
★ Add the basil and then stir in the drained pasta.

SUITABLE FROM 7 MONTHS

MAKES 3 PORTIONS

PREPARATION TIME: 10 MINUTES /
COOKING TIME: 10 MINUTES

SUITABLE FOR FREEZING

SUITABLE FROM 7 MONTHS

MAKES 2 PORTIONS

PREPARATION TIME: 7 MINUTES /
COOKING TIME: 7 MINUTES

SUITABLE FOR FREEZING

Fillet of fish with carrot, tomato and cheese sauce

150 g (5 oz) carrot, peeled and chopped
40 g (1½ oz) mini pasta shells
100 g (4 oz) fillet of plaice, cod
   or pollack, skinned
1 tbsp milk
a knob of butter
25 g (1 oz) unsalted butter
3 medium tomatoes, skinned,
   deseeded and chopped
40 g (1½ oz) Cheddar cheese, grated

★ Steam the carrot for about 10 minutes or until tender.
★ Cook the pasta according to the packet instructions. Drain.
★ Meanwhile, place the fish in a microwave dish, add the milk, dot with the knob of butter and cover, leaving an air vent. Microwave on High for about 1½ minutes. Alternatively, poach the fish in a saucepan of milk for a couple of minutes.
★ Melt the butter in a saucepan and cook the tomatoes for 3 minutes, then stir in the cheese until melted. Blend the fish together with the steamed sweet potato and tomato and cheese sauce. Stir in the cooked pasta.

Creamy spinach sauce

40 g (1½ oz) mini pasta shells
200 g (7 oz) fresh or 100 g (4 oz)
   frozen spinach
a knob of butter
2 tbsp milk
2 tbsp cream cheese
4 tbsp Parmesan, grated

★ Cook the pasta according to the packet instructions. Drain.
★ Carefully wash the spinach and cook with the water just clinging to its leaves in a pan over a low heat, stirring occasionally until wilted. Gently press out the excess water. If using frozen spinach, cook according to the packet directions.
★ Melt the butter in a small pan and sauté the spinach, then stir in the milk and cheeses. Transfer the mixture to a food processor and chop finely. Mix with the cooked pasta.

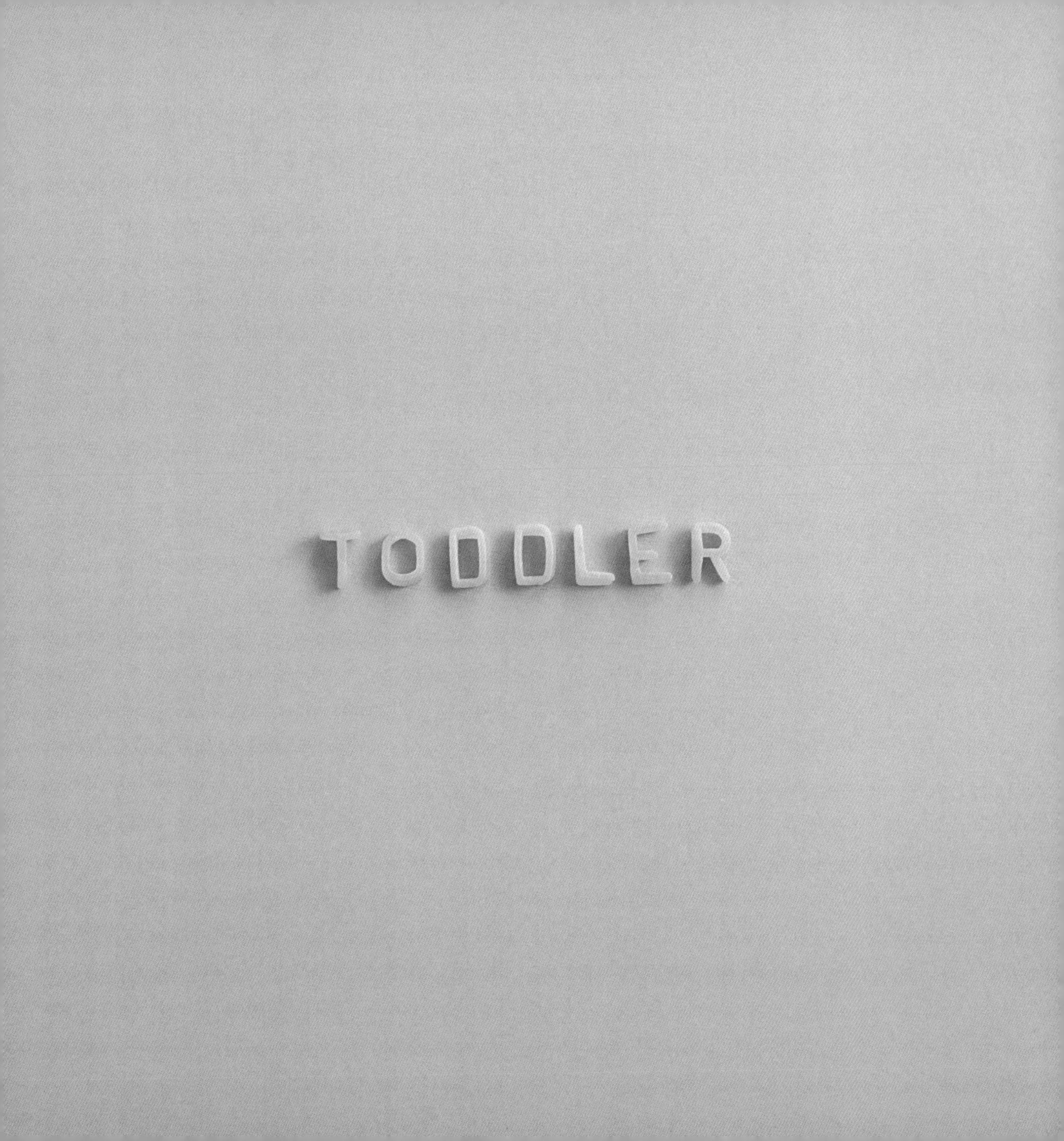
TODDLER

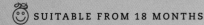

Chicken soup with alphabet pasta

According to food historians chicken soup was already being prescribed as a cure for the common cold in Ancient Egypt in the 10th century. Also known as Jewish penicillin, it is thought to be a natural remedy for colds and flu. Chicken soup is good for a sick child as it is easy to digest and will help to keep up their fluid levels.

15 g (½ oz) butter
2 shallots, finely chopped
1 medium carrot, peeled and diced
1 litre (1¾ pints) chicken stock
1 tsp soy sauce
1 large chicken breast fillet (approx. 175 g/6 oz), cut into small cubes
1 x 198 g can sweetcorn, drained
50 g (2 oz) small alphabet pasta shapes (or similar, such as stars)
100 g (3½ oz) frozen petit pois
chopped parsley, to serve (optional)
salt and freshly ground black pepper

★ Melt the butter in a large saucepan and sauté the shallots and carrot for 8–10 minutes until the shallots have softened. Add the stock and soy sauce, bring to the boil and boil for 5 minutes until the carrot is soft. Turn the heat down to very low, add the chicken and sweetcorn and cook very gently for 5 minutes until the chicken has cooked through. Try not to let the soup boil at all as the chicken can get a little tough.

★ Meanwhile, cook the pasta in well-salted boiling water according to the instructions on the packet. Drain.

★ Add the drained pasta plus the peas to the soup. Cook for a further 2–3 minutes, until the peas have just defrosted. Season well with a little salt and pepper. Ladle into warm bowls.

★ You can serve the soup garnished with a little chopped parsley if you like.

☺ SUITABLE FROM 2 YEARS

🥣 MAKES 4 PORTIONS

🕐 PREPARATION TIME: 10 MINUTES / COOKING TIME: 10 MINUTES

❄ NOT SUITABLE FOR FREEZING

Spaghetti with a mild curried chicken sauce

A mild fruity curry is popular with children. This one is very simple to make and can be served with pasta or rice.

250 g (9 oz) spaghetti
2 tbsp sunflower oil
125 g (4½ oz) onion, sliced
1 garlic clove, crushed
1½ tbsp korma curry paste
½ tbsp mango chutney
1 tbsp tomato purée
250 g (9 oz) chicken breast,
    cut into small strips
1 tbsp fresh chopped parsley
300 ml (10 fl oz) chicken stock
200 g (7 oz) tomatoes, skinned
    and coarsely chopped
100 g (3 oz) frozen peas
3 tbsp single cream
salt and freshly ground
    black pepper

★ Cook the spaghetti according to the instructions on the packet. Drain.

★ Heat the oil in a large saucepan and sauté the onion and garlic for 3–4 minutes. Add the korma paste, mango chutney and tomato purée and cook for 1 minute, stirring occasionally. Add the chicken and parsley and cook, stirring, for 2 minutes, then add the stock, chopped tomatoes and peas and cook for 3 minutes. Stir in the cream and season with a little salt and pepper.

★ Toss the drained pasta with the sauce.

Chicken and butternut squash pasta risotto

Orzo is pasta that looks like grains of rice, however you could make this using other small pasta shapes. Roasting the squash in the oven gives it a naturally sweet taste. If you prefer you could leave out the mushrooms and add some frozen peas towards the end instead.

350 g (12 oz) butternut squash, peeled, deseeded and sliced into small cubes
2 tbsp olive oil
100 g (4 oz) button mushrooms, sliced
250 g (9 oz) orzo or small pasta shapes
1.3 litres (2 pints) chicken stock
25 g (1 oz) butter
1 large onion, finely chopped
1 leek, finely chopped
1 garlic clove, crushed
2 tsp fresh thyme, chopped
150 g (5 oz) cooked chicken breast, sliced into small pieces
4 tbsp Parmesan cheese, grated
6 tbsp crème fraîche or single cream
salt and freshly ground black pepper

★ Preheat the oven to 200°C/400°F/Gas 6.
★ Toss the squash in 1 tablespoon of the olive oil and season. Place on a baking sheet and roast in the oven for 20–25 minutes until cooked and lightly golden brown.
★ Heat the remaining oil in a large saucepan and sauté the mushrooms for 5–6 minutes until golden brown. Remove from the pan and set aside.
★ Meanwhile, cook the orzo or pasta in the stock according to the instructions on the packet. Drain, reserving 2 tablespoons of the stock.
★ Melt the butter in the pan and add the onion, leek and garlic and fry for 5 minutes. Add the thyme and chicken and then the Parmesan, reserved stock and crème fraîche or cream. Simmer for 1 minute, then add the pasta, butternut squash and the mushrooms and toss together. Season well with black pepper.

SUITABLE FROM 18 MONTHS

MAKES 4 PORTIONS

PREPARATION TIME: 20 MINUTES / COOKING TIME: 15 MINUTES

MEATBALLS AND SAUCE SUITABLE FOR FREEZING

Turkey meatballs with spaghetti

You can also make this with minced chicken. When my son Nicholas was a toddler I couldn't get him to eat chicken, but as he liked apple I made mini chicken balls with grated apple – and he loved them. These meatballs also make good finger food served without the sauce and with the spaghetti on the side.

MEATBALLS
1 tbsp sunflower oil
1 medium onion, peeled and finely chopped
250 g (9 oz) minced turkey or chicken
40 g (1½ oz) ciabatta breadcrumbs
1 apple, peeled and grated
4 fresh sage leaves
1 tsp fresh thyme leaves or ¼ tsp dried thyme
flour, for dusting
salt and freshly ground black pepper

250 g (9 oz) spaghetti

SAUCE
2 tbsp sunflower oil
60 g (2½ oz) red onion
1 garlic clove, crushed
30 g (1 oz) SunBlush tomatoes, chopped
40 g (1½ oz) fresh chopped tomatoes
40 g (1½ oz) red pepper
1 x 400 g (14 oz) can chopped tomatoes

★ Preheat the oven to 180°C/350°F/Gas 4.
★ To make the turkey meatballs, heat the oil in a frying pan and sauté the onion for about 4 minutes. Allow to cool, then mix together the sautéed onion, minced turkey or chicken, breadcrumbs, grated apple, sage and thyme and season to taste. Put the mixture into a food processor and pulse for a couple of seconds. Using floured hands, form into about 12 meatballs. Arrange them on a baking sheet and cook for 10 minutes.
★ Meanwhile, cook the spaghetti according to the instructions on the packet. Drain.
★ To make the sauce, heat the oil in a saucepan and sauté the red onion for about 4 minutes, add the garlic and cook for ½ minute. Add the chopped SunBlush and fresh tomatoes and sauté for 3–4 minutes. Add the red pepper and sauté for 2 minutes. Add the canned tomatoes and cook for 5 minutes. Season to taste. Stir in the meatballs.
★ Toss with the drained spaghetti and carefully mix.

VARIATION: Try making these with the same quantity of minced beef instead of turkey.

 SUITABLE FROM 18 MONTHS

MAKES 4 PORTIONS

PREPARATION TIME: 8 MINUTES / COOKING TIME: 24 MINUTES

SUITABLE FOR FREEZING

Chicken Bolognese

Traditional Bolognese is made with minced beef, but a Bolognese made with minced chicken (preferably using thigh meat) is also delicious, and this is a popular dish with my children. Fresh thyme adds a nice flavour to the chicken. If you don't have sundried tomato paste you can use tomato purée.

200 g (7 oz) pasta shapes
(penne or fusilli)
1 tbsp light olive oil
1 small onion, finely chopped
1 small carrot, grated
1 apple, peeled and grated
250 g (9 oz) minced chicken
(I use chicken thigh meat)
1 garlic clove, crushed
300 ml (10 fl oz) passata
200 ml (7 fl oz) chicken stock
1 tsp sundried tomato paste or
purée
½ tsp fresh thyme leaves
salt and freshly ground
black pepper

★ Cook the pasta in a large pan of lightly salted boiling water according to the instructions on the packet. Drain.

★ Heat the oil in a saucepan. Add the onion and sauté for 5 minutes. Add the carrot and apple and sauté for another 5 minutes. Add the chicken and garlic and lightly fry while breaking up the mince. Add the passata, stock, sundried tomato paste or purée and thyme. Bring to the boil, then simmer, covered, for 10 minutes.

★ Season to taste and serve with the cooked pasta.

Three-cheese macaroni

This is a sort of cheat's way of making cheese sauce. If you can't find Taleggio, use Fontina cheese instead.

300 g (10½ oz) macaroni
125 g (4½ oz) mascarpone
150 ml (¼ pint) milk, plus
   1–2 tsp extra
125 g (4½ oz) Taleggio cheese,
   rind removed and cubed
50 g (2 oz) Gruyère, grated
½ tsp Dijon mustard
large pinch of grated nutmeg
100 g (3½ oz) grated Parmesan
salt and freshly ground black
   pepper
20 g (¾ oz) fresh breadcrumbs

★ Cook the macaroni according to the instructions on the packet. Drain and rinse with cold water. Leave to drain in a colander whilst you make the sauce.

★ Preheat the oven to 200°C/400°F/Gas 6.

★ Put the mascarpone and 100 ml (3½ fl oz) milk in a saucepan and heat gently until the mascarpone has melted. Add the Taleggio, Gruyère, mustard and nutmeg and heat, stirring the cheese until melted (be patient as it takes a few minutes).

★ Set aside a handful of the Parmesan and add the rest to the sauce. Stir until melted, then season with salt and black pepper and stir in the pasta and the remaining milk, then transfer to a baking dish.

★ Mix the reserved Parmesan and breadcrumbs and season with salt and pepper. Sprinkle this over the macaroni and cheese and bake for 20 minutes until golden on top and bubbling. (Brown it for a few minutes under a preheated grill if you wish.)

VARIATION: You can also add strips of ham or small broccoli florets that have been lightly blanched or steamed.

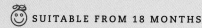

SUITABLE FROM 18 MONTHS

MAKES 4 PORTIONS

PREPARATION TIME: 8 MINUTES / COOKING TIME: 12 MINUTES

NOT SUITABLE FOR FREEZING

Oodles of noodles

Thin noodles with ribbons of colourful vegetables.

120 g (4½ oz) Chinese egg noodles
100 g (3½ oz) sliced onions
50 g (2 oz) carrots
50 g (2 oz) leeks
150 g (5½ oz) red, yellow and
**   orange peppers**
75 g (3 oz) baby courgettes
1 garlic clove, peeled and crushed
1½ tbsp sunflower oil
50 g (2 oz) beansprouts
1½ tbsp teriyaki sauce
salt and freshly ground black
**   pepper**

★ Cook the noodles according to the packet instructions.
★ Prepare the vegetables by cutting them into thin strips like ribbons – you can cut the carrots and courgettes simply using a vegetable peeler.
★ Heat the oil in a pan or a wok and stir-fry the onions, carrots and leeks for 5 minutes. Add the peppers, courgettes and garlic and cook for 5 minutes. Add the beansprouts and drained noodles. Pour over the teriyaki sauce. Season to taste and serve.

VARIATION: This is also wonderful with marinated chicken. To make the marinade, mix together in a bowl 2 tbsp soy sauce, 2 tbsp mirin, 1 tsp sugar and 1 tsp sesame oil. Cut 2 chicken breasts into thin strips and add to the marinade. Stir well then leave to marinate for 20 minutes. Sauté the chicken until sealed and cooked through (about 4–5 minutes). Add the cooked chicken at the point when you add the beansprouts and drained noodles.

Minestrone with pasta shells

You can make up your own combination of vegetables depending on what your child likes. If your child isn't keen on cannellini beans, leave them out, and if he doesn't like cabbage, substitute it with frozen peas instead.

125 g (4½ oz) mini pasta shells
2 tbsp sunflower oil
75 g (3 oz) chopped onion
75 g (3 oz) diced carrot
75 g (3 oz) diced celery
2 garlic cloves, chopped or crushed
75 g (3 oz) diced leek
1 litre (1¾ pints) vegetable stock, made with two stock cubes
40 g (1½ oz) fine green beans, cut into 1-cm (½-in) lengths
75 g (3 oz) diced courgettes
50 g (2 oz) finely shredded Savoy cabbage
75 g (3 oz) cannellini beans (from a can)
80 g (3 oz) fresh chopped tomatoes
1½ tbsp fresh pesto
salt and freshly ground black pepper

★ Cook the pasta shells in a large pan of lightly salted boiling water according to the instructions on the packet. Drain.
★ Heat the oil in a large saucepan and sauté the onion, carrot and celery for 2–3 minutes. Add the garlic and cook for ½ minute. Add the leek and sauté for 2 minutes.
★ Add the stock and simmer for 5 minutes. Add the green beans and cook for 1 minute. Add the courgettes, cabbage, drained pasta, beans and tomatoes and simmer for 2 minutes. Stir in the pesto and season to taste.

 SUITABLE FROM 1 YEAR

MAKES 4 PORTIONS

PREPARATION TIME: 12 MINUTES / COOKING TIME: 30 MINUTES

SUITABLE FOR FREEZING

Butternut squash gratin with penne

Butternut squash is rich in betacarotene and it tastes delicious mixed with a cheese sauce and pasta then baked in the oven with a golden breadcrumb topping.

**1 medium butternut squash
(approx. 850 g/2lb unpeeled,
prepared weight 450 g/1 lb)
175 g (6 oz) penne pasta
60 g (2 oz) fresh breadcrumbs**

**SAUCE
30 g (1 oz) butter, plus extra
for greasing
30 g (1 oz) flour
350 ml (12 fl oz) milk
55 g (2 oz) grated Gruyère cheese
100 g (3½ oz) grated Parmesan
4 tbsp double cream
salt and freshly ground black
pepper
a little grated nutmeg**

★ Cut the butternut squash in half, remove the seeds and fibre, peel, then chop into 2 cm cubes. Steam for about 8 minutes (not too long as it will be cooked again in the oven).

★ Cook the pasta in boiling water according to the instructions on the packet. Drain.

★ Preheat the oven to 200°C/400°F/Gas 6.

★ To make the sauce, melt the butter in a saucepan, and stir in the flour. Remove from the heat and whisk in the milk a little at a time to make a smooth sauce. Bring to the boil, then reduce the heat and stir until thickened. Remove from the heat and whisk in the Gruyère, a quarter of the Parmesan, and the cream. Season well with salt and pepper and nutmeg.

★ Lightly grease a 24 x 15cm Pyrex casserole or baking dish. Mix the pasta together with the butternut squash and cheese sauce and spoon into the dish.

★ Mix together the breadcrumbs and remaining Parmesan and season with a little salt and pepper. Sprinkle over the sauce and bake in the oven for 20–25 minutes until the top is golden and the sauce is bubbling.

★ Leave to stand for 15 minutes before serving.

VARIATION: If you like, add some diced cooked chicken to this.

SUITABLE FROM 1 YEAR

MAKES 4 PORTIONS

PREPARATION TIME: 12 MINUTES /
COOKING TIME: 28 MINUTES SAUCE

SUITABLE FOR FREZING

SUITABLE FROM 1 YEAR

MAKES 4 PORTIONS

PREPARATION TIME: 15 MINUTES /
COOKING TIME: 15 MINUTES

SAUCE SUITABLE FOR FREEZING

Hidden vegetable tomato sauce

1 tbsp olive oil
100 g (3½ oz) onion, chopped
40 g (1½ oz) leek, finely chopped
1 garlic clove, crushed
25 g (1 oz) red pepper, chopped
40 g (1½ oz) carrot, peeled and chopped
40 g (1½ oz) courgette, chopped
1½ tbsp sundried tomato purée
1½ tbsp tomato purée
1 tsp caster sugar
1 x 400 g can chopped tomatoes
150 ml (¼ pint) vegetable stock

★ Heat the oil in a saucepan and sauté the onion and leek for about 3 minutes, stirring occasionally. Add the garlic and sauté for 1 minute. Add the red pepper, carrot and courgette and cook for a further 3 minutes, stirring occasionally. Add the sundried tomato and tomato purées and caster sugar and cook, stirring, for about 1 minute. Add the chopped tomatoes and stock and simmer, uncovered, for 20 minutes, stirring occasionally.

Tuna, plum tomato and broccoli pasta

1 tbsp sunflower oil
1 red onion, finely chopped
100 g (3½ oz) button mushrooms,
    thinly sliced
100 g (3½ oz) SunBlush tomatoes
1½–2 tbsp balsamic vinegar
1 x 185 g can tuna in oil, drained
4 plum tomatoes, deseeded and
    roughly chopped
2 tbsp basil chopped
225 g (8 oz) fusilli pasta
100 g (3½ oz) tiny broccoli florets

★ Heat the oil in a deep saucepan, add the red onion and cook for 4–5 minutes. Add the mushrooms and SunBlush tomatoes and fry over a medium heat for another 4 minutes. Turn the heat down, then add the balsamic vinegar, tuna, tomatoes and basil.
★ Cook the pasta according to the instructions on the packet, adding the broccoli 3 minutes before the end of the cooking time. Add 3 tablespoons of the pasta water to the sauce, then drain the pasta and toss with the sauce.

⊙ SUITABLE FROM 1 YEAR

⊍ MAKES 4 PORTIONS

⊕ PREPARATION TIME: 15 MINUTES / COOKING TIME: 20 MINUTES

❋ NOT SUITABLE FOR FREEZING

Fusilli with salmon in a light cheese sauce with spring vegetables

This is a favourite recipe of mine; it's a delicious combination of spring vegetables and tender chunks of salmon. It makes a delicious meal for adults as well. The sauce couldn't be simpler – just stir together the ingredients and heat through.

200 g (7 oz) fusilli
2 tbsp light olive oil
1 onion, finely chopped
1 garlic clove, crushed
100 g (3½ oz) orange pepper,
    cut into strips
100 g (3½ oz) broccoli florets
1 medium courgette, sliced
    and cut into semi-circles
250 g (9 oz) salmon fillets
200 ml (7 fl oz) fish stock
150 g (5½ oz) crème fraîche
200 ml (7 fl oz) vegetable stock
150 g (5½ oz) tomatoes, skinned,
    deseeded and cut into chunks
75 g (3 oz) Parmesan cheese, grated
salt and freshly ground black
    pepper

★ Cook the fusilli according to the instructions on the packet.
★ Heat the oil in a heavy-based saucepan and sauté the onion and garlic for 3 minutes, stirring occasionally. Add the orange pepper, broccoli and courgette and sauté for 6–7 minutes until tender, stirring occasionally.
★ Meanwhile, cut the salmon into chunks, put in a saucepan, cover with fish stock and poach over a gentle heat for 3–4 minutes until cooked. Remove from the pan, strain and set aside.
★ Stir the crème fraîche and vegetable stock into the cooked vegetables and bring to a simmer. Stir in the chopped tomatoes and chunks of salmon and simmer for 2 minutes, then stir in the Parmesan and season to taste.
★ Toss the drained fusilli with the sauce, taking care not to break up the chunks of salmon.

Haddock and spinach pasta bake

Adding a little smoked haddock gives this dish a lovely flavour. Use undyed smoked haddock if you can.

225 g (8 oz) penne pasta
50 g (2 oz) butter
50 g (2 oz) plain flour
600 ml (1 pint) milk
1 tsp wholegrain mustard
1 tbsp fresh dill, chopped
100 g (4 oz) Parmesan
   cheese, grated
salt and freshly ground black
   pepper
200 g (7 oz) baby spinach
200 g (7 oz) fresh haddock, skinned
50 g (2 oz) smoked haddock,
   skinned
juice of ½ lemon

★ Preheat the oven to 200°C/400°F/Gas 6.
★ Cook the pasta in boiling salted water according to the instructions on the packet. Drain and refresh in cold water. Set aside.
★ Melt the butter in a saucepan, add the flour and stir over the heat for 2 minutes. Add the milk slowly, stirring until combined. Bring to the boil and simmer for 2 minutes until it has thickened. Add the mustard, dill and half of the Parmesan. Season well.
★ Heat a frying pan, add the spinach and fry over a high heat until wilted, then add to the sauce. Mix the penne with the sauce. Slice the haddock into 2 cm cubes and fold them into the mixture with the lemon juice.
★ Spoon into an ovenproof dish and sprinkle with the remaining Parmesan. Bake for 20–25 minutes until bubbling and lightly golden on top.

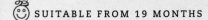

Salmon and orzo salad

This salad would be great for lunchboxes or picnics as well as a light lunch. The red pepper and cucumber add a good crunchy texture and the fresh herbs give the dish a nice summery flavour. Adults love this dish too!

300 g (10 oz) salmon fillet
a knob of butter
200 g (7 oz) orzo or small pasta shells
200 g (7 oz) frozen garden peas
1 red pepper, finely diced
½ cucumber, peeled, seeds removed and diced
1 small bunch spring onions, finely sliced
2 tbsp flat leaf parsley, chopped
2 tbsp dill, chopped
2 tbsp chives, chopped
2 tbsp olive oil
3 tbsp rice wine vinegar
1 tsp runny honey

★ Preheat the oven to 180°C/350°F/Gas 4.

★ Put the salmon fillet onto a piece of foil on a baking sheet with a knob of butter. Seal the foil to look like a parcel, then cook in the oven for 15 minutes until cooked through. Remove from the oven and leave to cool. Alternatively, you could cut the salmon into chunks, put it into a saucepan and poach in enough fish stock to cover the fish over a medium to low heat for about 7 minutes or until the fish flakes easily with a fork.

★ Cook the pasta in boiling salted water according to the instructions on the packet, and add the peas 4 minutes before the end of the cooking time. Drain and refresh in cold water.

★ Measure the remaining ingredients into a large bowl. Add the cooked pasta and peas, then flake in the cold salmon and any juices from the foil. Season well, then cover and chill for 30 minutes before serving.

SUITABLE FROM 2 YEARS

MAKES 4 PORTIONS

PREPARATION TIME: 10 MINUTES / COOKING TIME: 10 MINUTES

NOT SUITABLE FOR FREEZING

Teriyaki salmon with noodles

Mirin is a sweet Japanese rice wine used in cooking. It is delicious in marinades or dressings. You could also marinate the salmon for half an hour, thread it onto skewers and grill for 2 minutes each side. Oily fish such as salmon provides the best source of essential fatty acids which will help boost your child's brainpower.

TERIYAKI SAUCE
4 tbsp mirin
4 tbsp soy sauce
1 tsp cornflour
1 tbsp brown sugar
1 tbsp water

100 g (3½ oz) egg noodles
250 g (9 oz) salmon fillet, sliced
salt and freshly ground
    black pepper
2 tbsp sunflower oil
2 spring onions, chopped
100 g (3½ oz) sugar snap
    peas, sliced
100 g (3½ oz) beansprouts

★ First make the sauce. Mix all of the sauce ingredients together in a small bowl.

★ Cook the noodles in boiling water according to the instructions on the packet. Drain.

★ Slice the salmon into small cubes and place in a bowl with 2 tablespoons of the sauce. Toss together and season. Heat 1 tablespoon of oil in a wok and fry the salmon for 2 minutes on each side, then carefully transfer to a plate.

★ Heat the remaining oil. Fry the spring onions and sugar snap peas for 3 minutes. Add the noodles and beansprouts and fry for 2 minutes. Add the sauce and toss together. Add the salmon and carefully toss together.

Tomato and mascarpone sauce with tiger prawns

A simple but tasty tomato sauce you could also make without prawns.

1 tbsp olive oil
1 onion, finely chopped
2 garlic cloves, crushed
1 red chilli, deseeded and diced
1 x 400 g (14 oz) can chopped
   tomatoes
100 g (4 oz) mascarpone
225 g (8 oz) penne
225 g (8 oz) cooked tiger prawns
2 tbsp snipped chives
juice of ½ small lemon

★ Heat the oil in a saucepan and add the onion, garlic and chilli. Simmer for 5 minutes over a low heat. Add the tomatoes, cover and simmer for another 10 minutes. Add the mascarpone, then whiz in a food processor until smooth.
★ Put back into the saucepan and keep warm while you cook the penne in boiling salted water according to the instructions on the packet. Drain.
★ Add the prawns and chives to the sauce. Heat through, then add the lemon juice and cooked pasta.

SUITABLE FROM 18 MONTHS

MAKES 4 PORTIONS

PREPARATION TIME: 15 MINUTES / COOKING TIME: 15 MINUTES

SUITABLE FOR FREEZING

Sweet and sour meatballs

One of my signature recipes is my chicken and apple balls to which I add grated apple; I also add this to my meatballs to give them a good flavour and to keep them nice and moist. The sauce is quick and easy to prepare and can be served with pasta or rice.

MEATBALLS
1 tbsp oil
1 red onion, chopped
1 garlic clove, crushed
225 g (8 oz) lean minced beef
50 g (2 oz) apple, grated
30 g (1 oz) fresh breadcrumbs
1 tbsp parsley, chopped
2 tsp tomato ketchup
salt and freshly ground
   black pepper
2 spring onions, very finely
   sliced, to garnish (optional)
200 g (7 oz) medium egg noodles

SAUCE
2 tbsp soy sauce
4 tbsp tomato ketchup
1 tbsp rice wine vinegar
2 tsp brown sugar
150 ml (¼ pint) water
2 tsp cornflour mixed with
   a little water

★ Heat ½ tablespoon of the oil and sauté the onion for 5 minutes until softened but not coloured. Add the garlic and sauté for 1 minute, then set aside to cool.

★ Mix the mince, apple, breadcrumbs, parsley and ketchup together in a bowl.

★ Add half of the cold onion and garlic to the meatball mixture. Season with a little salt and pepper. Shape into 24 small meatballs. Heat the remaining ½ tablespoon of oil in a frying pan. Slowly cook the meatballs for about 10 minutes until golden and cooked through.

★ Cook the noodles in boiling salted water according to the instructions on the packet. Drain.

★ Add the sauce ingredients to the remaining onion and garlic. Bring to the boil and simmer for 2 minutes until it has reduced slightly. Mix the sauce with the noodles and serve topped with the meatballs and spring onions.

Veal escalopes with tomato and basil sauce

TOMATO SAUCE
3 tbsp olive oil
1 onion, chopped
2 garlic cloves, crushed
2 x 400 g (14 oz) cans chopped
    tomatoes
1 tbsp tomato purée
1 tbsp sundried tomato purée
1 tsp sugar
½ tsp dried thyme or 1 tsp fresh thyme
3 tbsp fresh basil, chopped
250 g (9 oz) spaghetti

salt and freshly ground black pepper
4 thin veal escalopes (about
    80–100 g/3–3½ oz each)
2 eggs, beaten
150 g (5½ oz) fresh white breadcrumbs
30 g (1 oz) Parmesan cheese, finely
    grated
2 tbsp parsley, chopped

★ Heat 1 tablespoon of olive oil in a saucepan. Add the onion and garlic and sauté for 2–3 minutes. Add the canned tomatoes, purées, sugar and thyme. Bring to the boil, cover with a lid and simmer for 20 minutes. Whiz the sauce to a purée using a hand blender.

★ Cook the pasta according to the instructions on the packet. Drain and add to the sauce with the basil.

★ If necessary, cover the veal with clingfilm and bash it out to a thickness of about 4 mm using a mallet. Season the veal and dip into the beaten egg. Mix together the breadcrumbs, Parmesan and parsley. Coat the veal in the breadcrumbs. Heat the remaining oil in a large non-stick frying pan. Fry the veal for 1½–2 minutes on both sides until golden and just cooked through. Remove from the heat and rest for 2 minutes.

★ Spoon some spaghetti onto a plate and serve with the veal on top.

Salami, red pepper and mozzarella pasta

Most children like salami, so here is a simple recipe that you can put together in about 15 minutes.

180 g (6 oz) pasta shells
2 tbsp olive oil
1 red pepper, finely diced
1 small garlic clove, crushed
50 g (2 oz) thinly sliced salami, roughly chopped
150 g (5½ oz) cherry tomatoes, chopped into 8
75 g (3 oz) mozzarella, cubed
grated Parmesan cheese, to serve

★ Cook the pasta in boiling salted water according to the instructions on the packet. Drain.
★ Heat the oil in a saucepan. Fry the pepper for 5 minutes, then add the garlic and salami. Fry for another 5 minutes. Add the drained pasta, cherry tomatoes and mozzarella and season. Serve with a little Parmesan cheese sprinkled on top.

Fusilli with chipolatas and sweet pepper

You can't go wrong with sausages and pasta. This would be a good dish to make if you have a group of children over as it is so quick and easy to prepare.

200 g (7 oz) fusilli pasta
2 tbsp sunflower oil
150 g (5½ oz) diced onion
5 g (¼ oz) chopped garlic
300 g (10½ oz) red, yellow and orange peppers, diced
400 g (14 oz) chipolata sausages (approx. 10)
120 g (4½ oz) cherry tomatoes, cut into quarters
leaves picked from 1 small bunch of thyme
50 g (2 oz) Cheddar cheese, grated

★ Cook the pasta in boiling salted water according to the instructions on the packet. Drain.
★ Preheat the oven to 200°C/400°F/Gas 6.
★ Heat the oil and sauté the onion, garlic and peppers for 5 minutes. Cook the sausages in the oven or under a grill. Allow to cool slightly and slice into chunks.
★ Mix the sausages, pasta, peppers, tomatoes and thyme together. Place in a casserole dish and top with the grated cheese. Bake for 20 minutes.

SUITABLE FROM 2 YEARS

MAKES 6 PORTIONS

PREPARATION TIME: 20 MINUTES / COOKING TIME: 1 HOUR AND 10 MINUTES

SUITABLE FOR FREEZING

Creamy beef cannelloni

This creamy beef cannelloni makes great comfort food. If you like you can freeze two cannelloni at a time in smaller dishes.

2 tbsp sunflower oil
1 large onion, roughly chopped
1 carrot, peeled and diced
375 g (12 oz) minced beef
2 garlic cloves, crushed
2 x 400 g (14 oz) cans chopped
   tomatoes
2 tbsp tomato purée
2 tsp sugar
salt and freshly ground black
   pepper
100 ml (3½ fl oz) double cream
small bunch of basil, chopped or
   some dried thyme
12 cannelloni tubes
50 g (2 oz) Cheddar cheese, grated

★ Preheat the oven to 200°C/400°F/Gas 6.

★ First make the filling. Heat 1 tablespoon of oil in a large pan. Add half the onion and the carrot and fry for a few minutes. Add the mince and brown over a high heat. Add 1 garlic clove, then a can of chopped tomatoes and 1 tablespoon of tomato purée. Stir together. Cover and simmer for 30–40 minutes until tender and most of the liquid has been absorbed. Stir in 1 teaspoon of sugar and season. Leave to cool.

★ Meanwhile, make the creamy tomato sauce. Heat the remaining oil in a pan. Add the remaining onion and garlic, sweat for a few minutes, then add the remaining can of tomatoes, purée and sugar. Cover and simmer for 15 minutes. Add the double cream and whiz using a hand blender until smooth.

★ Spoon a little creamy sauce in the base of a small ovenproof dish. Mix the basil into the cold beef mixture, then stuff the cannelloni tubes and lay in a single layer across the dish. Pour over the sauce and sprinkle with cheese. Bake for about 30 minutes until bubbling and golden on top.

Pork and beef meatballs with tagine sauce

It is important to introduce new flavours to your child, who will often have more sophisticated tastes than you might imagine. Try this mildly spiced Moroccan tagine. It makes a tasty meal that the whole family can enjoy.

TAGINE SAUCE
1 tbsp oil
1 small onion, finely chopped
150 g (5½ oz) butternut squash, coarsely grated
½ tsp fresh ginger, grated
½ tsp garam masala
½ tsp ground cinnamon
½ tsp ground coriander
1 x 400 g (14 oz) can chopped tomatoes
250 ml (9 fl oz) chicken stock
1 tsp sundried tomato purée
1 tsp honey

MEATBALLS
125 g (4½ oz) pork mince
125 g (4½ oz) beef mince
30 g (1 oz) fresh breadcrumbs
15 g (½ oz) Parmesan, grated
½ tsp chopped fresh coriander
1 egg yolk

200 g (7 oz) pasta

★ First make the tagine sauce. Heat the oil in a saucepan and add the onion and butternut squash. Sauté for 5 minutes, then add the ginger. Add the spices and fry for 1 minute. Add the remaining ingredients. Season and simmer for 10 minutes until the onion and squash are soft. Blend using a hand blender until smooth. Pour back into the saucepan.

★ To make the meatballs put all of the ingredients into a bowl. Season and mix together, then shape into 20 balls.

★ Bring the sauce to the boil, then drop in the meatballs in a single layer. Cover and simmer for 15 minutes.

★ Meanwhile, cook the pasta according to the instructions on the packet. Drain.

★ Serve the meatballs with the pasta.

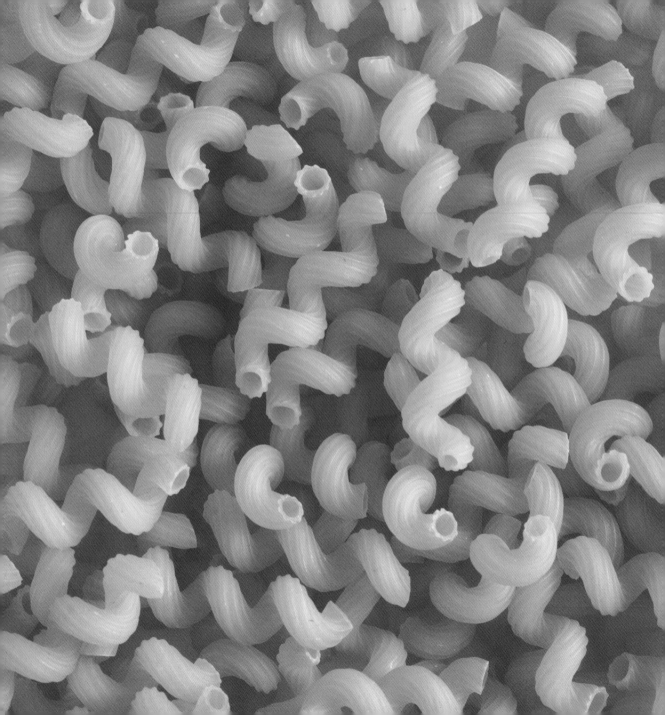

POULTRY
AND
PASTA

⊿ MAKES 5 PORTIONS

🕐 PREPARATION TIME: 15 MINUTES

⊙ COOKING TIME: 15 MINUTES

❄ SUITABLE FOR FREEZING

Corn and chicken laksa

Laksa comes from Singapore and Malaysia where 'slurping' your noodles
is considered essential!

150 g (5½ oz) thin egg noodles
2 tsp sunflower oil
1 small onion, finely chopped
1 garlic clove, crushed
1 tbsp mild curry paste
   (I used Patak's)
1 tbsp soft light brown sugar
400 ml/14 fl oz can coconut milk
250 ml/9 fl oz chicken stock
2 tsp soy sauce
½ tsp red chilli (just a hint,
   if it is too hot children
   may be put off)
1 x 198 g can sweetcorn
60 g (2½ oz) frozen peas
150 g (5½ oz) cooked chicken,
   shredded into small pieces
4 spring onions, thinly sliced,
   plus extra to serve (optional)
2 tsp lime or lemon juice
handful coriander leaves, to serve
   (optional)
sliced red chillies, to serve
   (optional)
lime quarters, to serve (optional)

★ Cook the noodles according to the instructions on the packet.
Drain.

★ Heat the oil and sauté the onion for 5–6 minutes, until soft. Add
the garlic, curry paste and sugar and cook for a further minute, then
add the coconut milk, chicken stock, soy sauce and red chilli. Bring
to the boil then drop in the corn and frozen peas, chicken and spring
onions. Simmer for 3 minutes, until everything is hot, then add the
lime or lemon juice.

★ Stir in the noodles, heat through and eat straightaway. You can
put out bowls of coriander leaves, extra spring onions, sliced chillies
and lime quarters so that everyone can help themselves to their
favourites.

Annabel's chicken pasta salad

Pasta salads make a nice change from sandwiches in lunchboxes and you could prepare this the night before and mix everything together in the morning. It's also good to have this made up in the fridge for your child to help himself to it after school.

DRESSING
1½ tbsp balsamic vinegar
½ tsp sugar
1 tbsp soy sauce
2 tbsp pesto
2 tbsp olive oil

150 g (5½ oz) cooked chicken
  breast, sliced into pieces
150 g (5½ oz) pasta shells
100 g (3½ oz) French beans,
  sliced into 3
2 carrots, grated
1 x 200 g (7 oz) can sweetcorn,
  drained
100 g (3½ oz) cherry tomatoes,
  quartered
salt and freshly ground black
  pepper

★ First make the dressing. Mix all of the dressing ingredients together and add the chicken. Leave to marinate in the fridge.
★ Cook the pasta in boiling salted water according to the instructions on the packet. Add the beans 4 minutes before the end of the cooking time. Drain and refresh in cold water.
★ Add the cold pasta and beans to the dressing along with the sliced chicken and all the other ingredients. Toss together and season well.

VARIATION: For a change, substitute the French beans with broccoli or cauliflower florets.

Annabel's pad thai

If your child is fussy don't just offer food you are sure that he or she will eat, as this can worsen the problem; keep trying new recipes. this tasty pad thai is usually very popular. You could make this vegetarian by replacing the chicken with more vegetables.

MARINADE
1 tbsp each soy sauce and sake
1½ tsp sugar
1½ tsp cornstarch

250 g (9 oz) chicken breast, cut into strips
175 g (6 oz) medium rice noodles
2½ tbsp sunflower oil, for frying
2 shallots, finely sliced, or 1 onion
¼ tsp caster sugar
1 garlic clove, crushed
½ tsp red chilli, sliced (optional)
1 leek, thinly sliced
100 g (3½ oz) broccoli, cut into small florets
295 g (10½ oz) beansprouts
2 eggs, lightly beaten with a little salt (cooked as a thin omelette and cut into strips)
2 tbsp rice wine vinegar
2 tbsp soy sauce
2 tsp fish sauce
2 tbsp sweet chilli sauce

★ Mix together the ingredients for the marinade and marinate the chicken for 30 minutes.

★ Cook the noodles according to the instructions on the packet.

★ Heat 1 tablespoon of the oil in a wok or large frying pan. Stir-fry the shallots or onion for about 3–4 minutes. Sprinkle with a generous pinch of caster sugar and stir-fry for 1 minute, then add the garlic and chilli (if using) and cook for 1 more minute. Add the chicken strips and stir-fry for 3–4 minutes until cooked. Remove from the wok and set aside.

★ Heat the remaining 1½ tablespoons of oil in the wok. Add the leek and stir-fry for 3 minutes. Add the broccoli and the beansprouts (reserving a couple of handfuls of beansprouts) and stir-fry for 4 minutes. Add the chicken, cooked drained noodles and strips of egg with the vinegar, soy, fish and sweet chilli sauces. Cook until the noodles are warmed through. Serve in bowls with the reserved raw beansprouts sprinkled over.

Fusilli with chicken and pesto

Pesto is a flavour that tends to be popular with children. It is easy to make your own pesto. Simply toast 60 g (2½ oz) pine nuts in a dry frying pan until golden, then leave to cool. Put 60 g (2½ oz) grated Parmesan, 1 garlic clove, a small bunch of basil, the cooled pine nuts and a pinch of sugar in a food processor and slowly add some olive oil while the motor is whizzing. Finish with a little water and some salt and pepper.

250 g (9 oz) fusilli pasta

a generous knob of butter
250 g (9 oz) cherry tomatoes,
    halved
½ tbsp sunflower oil
1 onion, sliced
1 garlic clove, crushed
200 g (7 oz) chicken breast,
    thinly sliced
1 tbsp balsamic vinegar
1 tbsp soy sauce
½ tbsp lemon juice
2 tbsp pesto
6 basil leaves
salt and freshly ground
    black pepper

★ Cook the pasta according to the instructions on the packet. Drain.
★ Heat the butter in a small saucepan and sauté the cherry tomatoes for 1 minute, then transfer to a small bowl and set aside.
★ Meanwhile, heat the oil in a wok and sauté the onion and garlic for 3 minutes, stirring occasionally, then add the chicken and continue to stir for 3 minutes. Add the balsamic vinegar, soy sauce, lemon juice and pesto and cook for 1 minute.
★ Add the cooked pasta to the onion and chicken mixture and mix in the sautéed cherry tomatoes and basil leaves and cook for 1 minute. Season with a little salt and pepper.

MAKES 4 PORTIONS

PREPARATION TIME: 8 MINUTES

COOKING TIME: 15 MINUTES

NOT SUITABLE FOR FREEZING

Chicken stir-fry with peanut butter sauce

Stir-fries are quick and easy to prepare and a good way to get your child to eat more vegetables if you mix them with a tasty sauce like this peanut butter one.

PEANUT BUTTER SAUCE
2 tbsp peanut butter
2 tsp brown sugar
1 tbsp soy sauce
150 ml (¼ pint) chicken stock
2 tsp rice wine vinegar

2 tbsp olive oil
1 large chicken breast, sliced
salt and freshly ground black
    pepper
1 small onion, thinly sliced
1 garlic clove, crushed
½ red chilli, diced
150 g (5½ oz) small broccoli florets
1 red pepper, thinly sliced
150 g (5½ oz) medium rice noodles
2 tsp lime juice

★ First make the sauce. Mix all of the ingredients together in a small bowl and set aside.
★ Heat 1 tablespoon of the oil. Season the chicken, then quickly brown over a high heat and place on a plate.
★ Heat the remaining oil. Add the onion, garlic and chilli. Sauté over a medium heat for 3–4 minutes. Add the broccoli and pepper and stir-fry for 4–5 minutes or until the broccoli is nearly cooked. Return the chicken to the pan with the sauce. Bring to the boil and season.
★ Cook the noodles in boiling salted water, drain, and add to the frying pan with the lime juice. Toss everything together and place in a serving dish.

- MAKES 4 PORTIONS
- PREPARATION TIME: 20 MINUTES
- COOKING TIME: 50 MINUTES
- SUITABLE FOR FREEZING

Chicken cannelloni

There are so many things that you can stuff inside cannelloni tubes, such as spinach and ricotta or Bolognese, but here's something a little different – tasty minced chicken with tomatoes covered with a creamy cheese sauce and a golden topping.

1 tbsp olive oil
1 onion, peeled and chopped
1 small garlic clove, crushed
40 g (1½ oz) mushrooms, chopped
½ tsp dried mixed herbs
225 g (8 oz) minced chicken
1 x 200 g (7 oz) can tomatoes
   or ½ x 400 g (14 oz) can
½ tbsp tomato ketchup

CHEESE SAUCE
30 g (1¼ oz) butter
30 g (1¼ oz) flour
½ tsp paprika
400 ml (14 fl oz) milk
100 g (3½ oz) Cheddar
   cheese, grated
8 no pre-cook cannelloni tubes

★ Heat the oil in a saucepan and sauté the onion and garlic for 2 minutes. Add the mushrooms, herbs and chicken and sauté for 3 minutes. Stir in the chopped tomatoes and ketchup and simmer for 20 minutes.

★ Preheat the oven to 180°C/350°F/Gas 4, then make the cheese sauce. Melt the butter, then stir in the flour and paprika and cook for 1 minute. Gradually whisk in the milk. Bring to the boil and then simmer, stirring, until thickened. Stir in 50 g (2 oz) of the grated Cheddar.

★ Stuff the cannelloni tubes with the chicken filling and arrange them in a shallow ovenproof dish. Pour over the cheese sauce, sprinkle with the remaining Cheddar cheese and bake in the oven for 25 minutes.

Confit duck and tomato ragu rigatoni

Confit duck is cooked duck legs, which you can buy canned in large supermarkets. It's very tasty and easy to use.

160 g (5½ oz) rigatoni pasta
170 g (6 oz) confit duck
2 tbsp sunflower oil
130 g (4½ oz) onion, diced
2 garlic cloves, chopped
600 g (1¼ lb) fresh tomatoes, chopped
2 sprigs fresh oregano, chopped
salt and freshly ground black pepper

★ Preheat the oven to 160°C/325°F/Gas 3.
★ Cook the rigatoni in boiling salted water according to the instructions on the packet. Drain.
★ Flake the duck meat off the duck legs and warm in the oven for 15–20 minutes.
★ Heat the oil in a saucepan and sauté the onion and garlic for 5 minutes. Add the fresh chopped tomatoes and simmer for 10 minutes. Fold in the duck and oregano. Season to taste.
★ Serve the sauce with the drained pasta.

Singapore noodles

Children often have more adventurous tastes than we might imagine and I find that they enjoy oriental-style recipes like these noodles, particularly if you give them 'child-friendly' chopsticks that are joined at the top to eat them with.

MARINADE
2 tsp each soy sauce and sake
1½ tsp sugar
1½ tsp cornstarch

200 g (7 oz) chicken breast,
   cut into strips
100 g (3½ oz) fine Chinese noodles
2 tbsp vegetable oil
150 g (5½ oz) carrots, cut into
   matchsticks
1 garlic clove, crushed
½ red chilli, deseeded and finely
   sliced
1 heaped tbsp korma curry paste
   (I used Patak's)
100 ml (3½ fl oz) coconut milk
50 ml (2 fl oz) strong chicken stock
   (made with 2 tsp of chicken
   stock powder)
4 drops fish sauce
50 g (2 oz) frozen peas
50 g (2 oz) canned sweetcorn

★ Mix together the ingredients for the marinade and marinate the chicken for about 30 minutes.

★ Cook the noodles in boiling water according to the instructions on the packet. Drain.

★ Heat the oil in a wok and stir-fry the carrots for 4 minutes. Add the garlic and chilli and stir-fry for 30 seconds. Add the chicken and stir-fry until just cooked. Stir in the korma curry paste, coconut milk, chicken stock and fish sauce. Then stir in the peas and sweetcorn and cook for about 3 minutes or until both the chicken and peas are cooked. About 2 minutes before the end of the cooking time, stir in the drained noodles.

Annabel's pasta salad with marinated chicken and roasted peppers

This is one of my favourite salads. Roasting peppers in the oven gives them a deliciously sweet flavour. You could marinate 2 uncooked chicken breasts for about 10 minutes in some olive oil, rice wine vinegar and pesto, then griddle the chicken and serve this as a warm salad.

1 red pepper, sliced in half and deseeded
1 yellow pepper, sliced in half and deseeded
2 tsp Dijon mustard
4 tbsp olive oil
3 tbsp rice wine vinegar
1 tbsp green pesto
2 cooked chicken breasts, thinly sliced
2 tbsp parsley, chopped
2 spring onions, finely sliced
½ garlic clove, crushed
150 g (5 oz) fusilli, cooked and refreshed in cold water
50 g (2 oz) pea shoots or watercress
salt and freshly ground black pepper

★ Preheat the oven to 200°C/400°F/Gas 6.

★ Place the red and yellow peppers, cut-side down, on a baking sheet. Roast in the oven for 20–25 minutes until soft and the skins are dark brown. Remove from the oven, place in a bowl, cover with cling film and leave to cool. Once cool enough to handle, remove the skins and slice the flesh into thin strips.

★ Mix together the Dijon mustard, oil, rice wine vinegar and pesto in a large bowl. Add the chicken, parsley, spring onions, garlic and cooked pasta and toss together with the peppers. Leave to marinate in the fridge for 1 hour.

★ Scatter a few of the pea shoots or some of the watercress on the base of a serving plate. Roughly chop the remaining leaves and fold into the salad with some salt and pepper. Spoon the salad onto the serving plate.

Chicken noodle salad with peanut dressing

This delicious peanut dressing combines well with shredded chicken, rice noodles and crunchy vegetables.

500 ml (18 fl oz) chicken stock
2 large chicken thighs
125 g (4½ oz) thin rice noodles
vegetable oil, for tossing
¼ Chinese cabbage, finely
    shredded
1 carrot, peeled and cut into
    matchsticks
¼ cucumber, cut into matchsticks
4 spring onions, sliced

DRESSING
50 g (2 oz) peanut butter
1 tbsp sweet chilli sauce
4 tbsp chicken stock (from
    the poached chicken)
2 tbsp rice wine vinegar
½ tsp caster sugar
1 tbsp vegetable oil

★ Bring the chicken stock to the boil in a large saucepan, add the chicken thighs, cover with a lid and simmer for 15 minutes. Lift out the chicken with a slotted spoon and set aside to cool.

★ Return the stock to the boil, turn off the heat and add the rice noodles. Leave to soak for about 4 minutes or until tender, then drain, reserving the chicken stock. Rinse the noodles under the tap and leave to drain. Toss with a little oil.

★ Remove the skin from the chicken thighs and shred the flesh. Add to the noodles together with the shredded Chinese cabbage, carrot, cucumber and spring onions.

★ Mix together all the ingredients for the dressing and toss with the salad.

⊔ MAKES 6 PORTIONS

PREPARATION TIME: 12 MINUTES

COOKING TIME: 40 MINUTES

SUITABLE FOR FREEZING

Turkey pasta bake with creamy Parmesan and tomato sauce

This is a wonderful recipe for using up leftover roast chicken or turkey. Turkey and penne are mixed together with a tasty tomato sauce made from sweet pepper and SunBlush tomatoes, and covered in a creamy Parmesan sauce.

225 g (8 oz) penne pasta

TOMATO SAUCE
2 tbsp olive oil
1 onion, chopped
1 red pepper, deseeded and diced
1 garlic clove, crushed
1 x 400 g (14 oz) can chopped tomatoes
2 tsp balsamic vinegar
1 tbsp tomato purée
2 tbsp fresh chopped basil
85 g (3 oz) SunBlush tomatoes,
   snipped into pieces
1 tsp dried oregano
250 g (9 oz) cooked turkey or
   chicken, sliced into strips

WHITE SAUCE
45 g (1½ oz) butter
45 g (1½ oz) flour
400 ml (14 fl oz) hot chicken stock
100 ml (3½ fl oz) double cream
100 g (3½ oz) Parmesan cheese, grated

★ Preheat the oven to 180°C/350°F/Gas 4.

★ Cook the penne in boiling salted water according to the instructions on the packet. Drain and refresh in cold water.

★ Make the tomato sauce. Heat the oil in a saucepan. Add the onion, pepper and garlic and simmer for 8 minutes until just tender. Add the tomatoes, vinegar and tomato purée and simmer for 5 minutes. Add the tarragon, SunBlush tomatoes and oregano, then the turkey or chicken and the penne. Mix together, then spoon into a shallow ovenproof dish.

★ Make the white sauce. Melt the butter in a saucepan. Add the flour and stir over the heat for 1 minute. Add the stock, slowly stirring until thickened. Stir in the cream and 50 g (2 oz) of the Parmesan. Spoon over the pasta and sprinkle the remaining Parmesan on top.

★ Bake for 15–20 minutes until hot, then finish off under a preheated grill for about 3 minutes until golden.

Caesar salad with chicken pasta and crispy bacon

Caesar salad is a classic favourite, but to give it more child appeal why not add some pasta? Some children are not keen on avocado (I think they don't like the mushy texture), so if your child doesn't like it, leave it out.

DRESSING
2 tsp Dijon mustard
1 tbsp white wine vinegar
1 small garlic clove, crushed
2 tbsp lemon juice
6 tbsp light mayonnaise
6 tbsp cold water
½ tsp Worcestershire sauce
30 g (1 oz) Parmesan cheese, finely grated
salt and freshly ground black pepper

SALAD
150 g (5½ oz) bow tie pasta
200 g (7 oz) cooked chicken breast, sliced into small cubes
50 g (2 oz) cherry tomatoes, halved
1 small avocado, cubed
2 tbsp chives, chopped
50 g (2 oz) Parmesan cheese, coarsely grated
150 g (5½ oz) cooked crispy bacon, roughly chopped

★ First, make the dressing. Measure the mustard, vinegar, garlic and lemon juice into a small bowl. Whisk together, then add the remaining dressing ingredients and whisk until smooth. Season to taste.

★ Mix all of the salad ingredients together in a large bowl. Spoon over the dressing and mix together.

🥣 MAKES 4 PORTIONS

🕐 PREPARATION TIME: 15 MINUTES

☉ COOKING TIME: 25 MINUTES

❄ NOT SUITABLE FOR FREEZING

Pasta pesto chicken with parma ham

Tender chicken breasts with mozzarella and pesto wrapped in Parma ham and served on a bed of curly pasta shapes. A delicious family dish which would also make a stunning dish for a special supper party.

1 x 250 g (9 oz) mozzarella ball
3–4 tbsp fresh green pesto
4 x small chicken breasts, skinned
bunch of basil
4 slices Parma ham
4 small bunches cherry tomatoes
   on the vine
1 tbsp runny honey
200 g (7 oz) chifferti rigati pasta
1 tbsp olive oil
1 onion
2 garlic cloves, crushed
4 tbsp crème fraiche
1 tbsp lemon juice

★ Preheat the oven to 200°C/400°F/Gas 6.

★ Slice the mozzarella in half lengthways, then slice each half into 4 slices. Spread 1 teaspoon of pesto over each chicken breast. Put 2 slices of mozzarella on top and 1 basil leaf. Wrap each breast in 1 slice of Parma ham. Arrange on a baking sheet. Put the tomatoes around the chicken. Drizzle the honey over the ham. Roast for 20–25 minutes or until the ham is crisp and the chicken is cooked through.

★ Meanwhile, cook the pasta in boiling salted water according to the instructions on the packet. Drain.

★ Heat the oil in a saucepan, add the onion and garlic and sauté for 4–5 minutes until soft. Add the pasta, crème fraîche, lemon juice and remaining basil. Stir in 2 tablespoons of pesto. Spoon the pasta onto a plate. Place a chicken breast on top and garnish with the tomatoes.

MAKES 4 PORTIONS

PREPARATION TIME: 10 MINUTES

COOKING TIME: 15 MINUTES

NOT SUITABLE FOR FREEZING

Fusilli with chicken and spring vegetables

SunBlush tomatoes are not sundried tomatoes, which are quite tough; they are soft and moist and good to use with fresh tomatoes to add more flavour.

1 tbsp olive oil
1 red onion, chopped
1 red pepper, diced
70g (3 oz) pancetta
1 large chicken breast, sliced
  into thin strips
4 large tomatoes, deseeded
  and roughly chopped
100 g (3½ oz) SunBlush
  tomatoes
4 tbsp crème fraîche
225 g (8 oz) fusilli pasta
100 g (3½ oz) frozen peas

★ Heat the oil in a frying pan, add the onion and pepper and sauté for 4 minutes until just starting to soften. Add the pancetta and chicken and sauté until the chicken is cooked and the pancetta is crispy. Turn down the heat, then add the tomatoes, SunBlush tomatoes and crème fraîche.

★ Cook the pasta according to the instructions on the packet. Add the peas 3 minutes before the end of the cooking time. Add 3 tablespoons of the pasta water to the sauce before draining and tossing in the sauce.

Open chicken and broccoli lasagne

2 large chicken breasts
1 garlic clove, crushed
1 tbsp oil
sprig of thyme
150 g (5½ oz) broccoli florets
6 fresh lasagne sheets

CHEESE SAUCE
20 g (¾ oz) butter
20 g (¾ oz) flour
300 ml (10 fl oz) milk
50 g (2 oz) grated mature Cheddar
50 g (2 oz) grated Gruyère
30 g (1 oz) grated Parmesan
½ tsp Dijon mustard
a little grated nutmeg
salt and freshly ground
**   black pepper**

★ Cut the chicken breasts in half horizontally. Mix together the garlic, oil and thyme and rub over the chicken. Leave to marinate for 10 minutes while you make the cheese sauce.
★ To make the cheese sauce, melt the butter, stir in the flour and cook for 1 minute. Gradually stir in the milk. Bring to the boil and cook, stirring over a medium heat until the sauce is thickened and smooth. Remove from the heat and stir in the Cheddar, Gruyère, half the Parmesan and the mustard. Add a little nutmeg and season to taste. Keep warm.
★ Heat a griddle and brush with oil. Season the chicken and griddle the chicken for 3–4 minutes on each side. Alternatively, stir-fry the chicken.
★ Cook the broccoli in boiling salted water or steam for 4 minutes until tender. Blanch the lasagne sheets in boiling salted water. Cut each sheet in half.
★ Assemble the lasagne on 4 heatproof plates. Put one square of pasta on each plate. Slice the chicken and divide half of it among the plates, along with the broccoli and one-third of the cheese sauce. Repeat with another layer of pasta, chicken, broccoli and sauce. Top each with a square of pasta and spoon over the remaining sauce. Sprinkle over the remaining Parmesan and grill each one for 2–3 minutes or reheat slightly and brown the Parmesan.
★ Serve immediately.

Marinated chicken pasta stir-fry

A simple and quick dish of chicken marinated in soy sauce and sake (a sweet Japanese rice wine), stir-fried with a selection of vegetables, then finished off with a tasty sauce made from soy, plum and oyster sauces.

MARINADE
1 tbsp soy sauce
1 tbsp sake
1 tsp sesame oil
1 tsp cornflour
½ tsp sugar

1 large chicken breast, sliced into
   thin strips
2 tsp sesame oil
½ onion, sliced
1 red pepper, sliced
100 g (3½ oz) broccoli florets
100 g (3½ oz) bow-tie pasta, cooked
   and refreshed in cold water
4 spring onions, sliced
100 g (3½ oz) beansprouts

STIR-FRY SAUCE
1 tbsp soy sauce
1 tbsp plum sauce
1 tbsp oyster sauce
150 ml (¼ pint) chicken stock (cold)
2 tsp cornflour

★ First make the marinade. Measure all of the ingredients into a bowl and add the chicken. Toss together, then leave to marinate in the fridge for 30 minutes.

★ Heat the 2 teaspoons of sesame oil in a wok. Add the onion and pepper and stir-fry for 2 minutes. Add the chicken and marinade and fry for 2 minutes.

★ Mix together all of the sauce ingredients, then pour over the chicken. Add the broccoli, cooked pasta and spring onions and simmer for 4 minutes. Add the beansprouts. Toss together and serve at once.

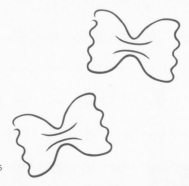

MAKES 4 PORTIONS

PREPARATION TIME: 10 MINUTES, PLUS 30 MINUTES MARINATING

COOKING TIME: 15 MINUTES

SUITABLE FOR FREEZING

Honey and mustard chicken with peppers

Mild grainy mustard and honey add a delicious flavour to the marinated chicken. If you prefer, you can use half-fat crème fraîche.

2 large chicken breasts, skinned and sliced into thin strips
1 tsp paprika
2 tsp grainy mustard
2 tsp runny honey
1 tbsp Worcestershire sauce
2 tbsp oil
salt and freshly ground black pepper
1 small onion, finely chopped
1 yellow pepper, diced
75 ml (2½ fl oz) chicken stock
100 ml (3½ fl oz) crème fraîche
100 g (3½ oz) cherry tomatoes, halved
pinch of sugar

200 g (7 oz) cooked penne pasta, to serve
chopped parsley, to serve

★ Put the chicken strips into a bowl. Measure the paprika, mustard, honey and Worcestershire sauce on top and toss together. Cover and marinate in the fridge for 30 minutes.
★ Heat 1 tablespoon of oil in a non-stick frying pan. Season the chicken, then quickly brown it and transfer to a plate.
★ Heat the remaining oil. Add the onion and pepper and sauté for 4–5 minutes until really soft. Add any remaining marinade from the bowl to the pan. Add the stock, bring up to the boil, then stir in the crème fraîche. Return the chicken to the pan and simmer for 5 minutes until cooked through. Just before serving, stir in the cherry tomatoes and sugar.
★ Serve with penne and chopped parsley.

MEATY MENUS

MAKES 12 PORTIONS

PREPARATION TIME: 12 MINUTES

COOKING TIME: 40 MINUTES

SUITABLE FOR FREEZING

Bolognese bake

This could also be served without the cheese as a spaghetti Bolognese.

2 tbsp oil
1 medium red onion, finely chopped
½ red pepper, diced
1 medium carrot, diced
½ celery stick, finely chopped
60 g (2½ oz) small courgette,
  chopped
30 g (1 oz) apple, grated
1 garlic clove, crushed
1 x 400 g (14 oz) can chopped
  tomatoes
100 ml (3½ fl oz) beef stock
450 g (1 lb) lean minced beef
2 tbsp tomato purée
3 tbsp tomato ketchup
½ tsp dried thyme
¼ tsp black pepper and some salt,
  to taste
250 g (9 oz) pasta twirls or
  corkscrews
50 g (2 oz) grated Cheddar
  (optional)

★ Heat the oil in a large saucepan and sauté the vegetables and apple for 10–15 minutes, stirring frequently until soft and slightly coloured, then add the garlic and cook for 1 minute. Transfer to a blender and add the tomatoes and stock and whiz until smooth. Return to the pan.

★ Brown the mince in a non-stick pan (you don't need any oil) and add to the vegetable and tomato mixture in the saucepan along with the tomato purée, ketchup, thyme and black pepper. Mix together, bring to a boil and simmer for 20–25 minutes. Season to taste.

★ Meanwhile, cook the pasta according to the instructions on the packet. Drain, and mix with the sauce. Preheat the grill. Place the pasta and sauce in a large baking dish, sprinkle over the cheese, if using, and brown under the grill.

Italian meatballs with penne and tomato sauce

It's a good idea to keep a supply of home-cooked meals in the freezer and these meatballs in tomato sauce are perfect for freezing in sets of six. You could serve these with any type of pasta, but it's best to cook the pasta fresh.

MEATBALLS
225 g (8 oz) lean minced beef
2 tsp green pesto
50 g (2 oz) grated apple
25 g (1 oz) fresh breadcrumbs
½ small garlic clove, crushed
15 g (½ oz) grated Parmesan
2 tsp fresh basil, chopped
1 egg yolk

TOMATO SAUCE
1 tbsp oil
1 onion, chopped
½ garlic clove, crushed
2 x 400 g (14 oz) tin chopped tomatoes
2 tsp sugar
½ tsp balsamic vinegar
1 tbsp tomato purée
2 tbsp fresh basil, chopped
salt and freshly ground black pepper

175 g (6 oz) penne

★ First, make the meatballs. Put all the ingredients into a bowl, mix together using your hands and form into 24 mini meatballs. Put in the fridge while you make the sauce.

★ Heat the oil in a pan and fry the onion and garlic for 2–3 minutes. Add the tomatoes, sugar, balsamic vinegar and purée. Bring to the boil then simmer, uncovered, for 10–15 minutes or until the sauce has reduced and thickened slightly. Season with a little salt and black pepper.

★ Add the meatballs, coat them in the tomato sauce, cover and simmer for 10–12 minutes or until the meatballs are cooked through.

★ Cook the pasta in a saucepan of boiling salted water according to the instructions on the packet. Drain.

★ Mix the pasta and sauce together and sprinkle with basil, if you wish (although some children don't like to see green bits in the sauce).

MAKES 4 PORTIONS

PREPARATION TIME: 15 MINUTES

COOKING TIME: 25 MINUTES

SUITABLE FOR FREEZING (STROGANOFF ONLY)

Beef stroganoff with tagliatelle

I buy tail fillet from my butcher to make stroganoff; it's cheaper than normal fillet steak and tastes the same, so it's perfect. Traditionally, you make this with button mushrooms, but chestnut mushrooms are also good, or if you are feeling extravagant you could use shitake mushrooms.

1–2 tbsp olive oil
150 g (5½ oz) mushrooms,
    thinly sliced
225 g (8 oz) fillet or sirloin
    steak, thinly sliced
a large knob of butter
3 small shallots, thinly sliced
1 garlic clove, crushed
½ tsp thyme leaves
250 ml (9 fl oz) beef stock
200 ml (7 fl oz) double cream
½ tsp Dijon mustard
2 tsp soy sauce
1 tsp sugar
freshly ground black pepper,
    to taste
small squeeze of lemon juice,
    to taste
200 g (7 oz) tagliatelle
parsley, to serve

★ Heat 2 teaspoons of oil in a wok or a large frying pan. Sauté the mushrooms for 5–6 minutes until golden brown. Transfer to a bowl. Heat another teaspoon of oil in the pan and fry the steak quickly (about 1–2 minutes) until browned. Don't overcrowd the pan – it is best to cook the meat in 2–3 batches or else the beef will stew in its own juices. Transfer the beef to the bowl with the mushrooms.

★ Turn down the heat to low. Melt the butter and gently cook the shallots for 8–10 minutes until soft. Add the garlic and thyme and cook for 1 minute. Add the beef stock and boil for 2–3 minutes until reduced by half. Whisk in the cream, mustard, soy sauce and sugar and boil for 2–3 minutes until thick enough to coat the back of a spoon. Reduce the heat to low and add the mushrooms and beef. Season to taste with black pepper and lemon juice (you probably won't need to add salt).

★ Cook the tagliatelle in a pan of boiling water according to the instructions on the packet. Drain and transfer to plates. Spoon over the sauce. Serve sprinkled with parsley.

MAKES 4 PORTIONS

PREPARATION TIME: 20 MINUTES

COOKING TIME: 40 MINUTES

SUITABLE FOR FREEZING (WITHOUT THE MOZZARELLA)

Mozzarella and meatball pasta bake

Pesto is a flavour that children tend to really like, so here I've mixed pesto with my meatballs. Like strawberries and cream, pesto and mozzarella are great partners, so I have added some diced mozzarella to the tomato sauce.

225 g (8 oz) fusilli pasta

SAUCE
1 tbsp light olive oil
1 large red onion, chopped
2 garlic cloves, crushed
2 x 400 g (14 oz) tins chopped tomatoes
1 tbsp tomato purée
1 tsp sugar
3 tbsp fresh basil, chopped
250 g (9 oz) mozzarella ball, drained and cut into small cubes
25 g (1 oz) Parmesan cheese, grated

MEATBALLS
225 g (8 oz) minced beef
3 tbsp green pesto
50 g (2 oz) fresh breadcrumbs
25 g (1 oz) Parmesan cheese
1 egg yolk
salt and freshly ground black pepper

★ Preheat the oven to 200°C/400°F/Gas 6.
★ Cook the pasta in boiling salted water until just cooked. Drain and refresh in cold water. Set aside.
★ Heat the oil in a saucepan and add the onion and garlic. Cook for 5 minutes over a low heat, then add the tomatoes. Bring to the boil, then simmer, uncovered, for 15 minutes until the sauce has reduced and thickened. Add the tomato purée and sugar and stir in the basil.
★ Mix the mince with 1 tablespoon of pesto, the breadcrumbs, Parmesan, egg yolk and seasoning. Shape the mince mixture into 24 small balls. Heat a non-stick frying pan and fry the meatballs until browned.
★ Mix together the pasta, tomato sauce, half the mozzarella and all the meatballs, then spoon into an ovenproof dish. Blob the remaining 2 tablespoons of pesto over the pasta. Sprinkle over the remaining mozzarella and Parmesan. Bake for 20–25 minutes until golden brown and heated through.

MAKES 4 PORTIONS

PREPARATION TIME: 8 MINUTES

COOKING TIME: 12 MINUTES

SUITABLE FOR FREEZING

MAKES 4 PORTIONS

PREPARATION TIME: 5 MINUTES

COOKING TIME: 10 MINUTES

NOT SUITABLE FOR FREEZING

Sausage, sage and red onion fusilli

160 g (5½ oz) fusilli pasta
2 tbsp sunflower oil
300 g (10½ oz) sliced red onion
1 tbsp honey
20 g (¾ oz) brown sugar
8 Cumberland or Lincolnshire
   sausages
10 fresh sage leaves
salt and freshly ground black pepper

★ Cook the fusilli in boiling salted water according to the instructions on the packet.
★ Heat the oil in a pan and sauté the onion. Add the honey and brown sugar and cook for 10 minutes until caramelised.
★ Cook the sausages in a frying pan then slice them into pieces. Chop the sage leaves. Mix together the pasta, caramelised onion, sausages and sage leaves. Season to taste and serve.

Penne carbonara

200 g (7 oz) penne pasta
1 tbsp sunflower oil
150 g (5½ oz) bacon lardons
125 ml (4 fl oz) double cream
125 ml (4 fl oz) chicken stock
30 g (1 oz) Parmesan, finely grated
1 egg yolk
salt and freshly ground black pepper

★ Cook the pasta in boiling water according to the instructions on the packet.
★ Heat the oil in a small frying pan and fry the bacon for 5–8 minutes until cooked and crispy. Drain on kitchen paper.
★ Put the remaining ingredients into a bowl and mix together. Drain the pasta and tip it into the dry pan. Add the cream mixture and bacon and gently heat for 2–3 minutes or until the sauce is hot and has thickened. Season to taste.

Spaghetti bolognese with pesto

Spaghetti Bolognese is always a crowd-pleaser, and this has a bit of a twist as I add some chopped SunBlush tomatoes and pesto.

2 tbsp sunflower oil
75 g (3 oz) onion, peeled and
    chopped
75 g (3 oz) leek, diced
2 garlic cloves, finely chopped
500 g (18 oz) lean minced beef
100 ml (3½ fl oz) beef stock
100 g (3½ oz) fresh tomatoes,
    chopped
1 x 400 g (14 oz) tin chopped
    tomatoes
100 g (3½ oz) SunBlush
    tomatoes, chopped
2 tbsp pesto
350 g (12 oz) spaghetti
salt and freshly ground black
    pepper

★ Heat the oil in a large heavy-based saucepan. Sauté the onion and leek for about 5 minutes until softened but not coloured. Add the garlic and cook for 1 minute. Add the mince and sauté, stirring occasionally, until browned. Stir in the stock and fresh, tinned and SunBlush tomatoes. Simmer for 35–40 minutes.

★ Meanwhile, cook the spaghetti according to the instructions on the packet. Drain.

★ Stir the pesto into the sauce, season to taste and toss with the pasta.

MAKES 4 PORTIONS

PREPARATION TIME: 12 MINUTES

COOKING TIME: 12 MINUTES

IF YOU FREEZE THE BEEF FOR 1 HOUR IT WILL MAKE SLICING IT EASIER.

Stir-fried beef with noodles

This is one of my favourite recipes which is loved by my children and often requested by them when I ask what they would like for supper. This sauce has a lovely rich Japanese-style flavour.

300 g (10 oz) sirloin, rump
    or fillet steak
2 eggs
4 level tbsp cornflour
a pinch of salt
1 medium carrot, peeled
2 medium courgettes, peeled
sunflower oil
4 spring onions, sliced
1 red chilli, deseeded and chopped
1 garlic clove, peeled and crushed
100 g (4 oz) medium egg noodles,
    cooked according to the
    instructions on the packet

SAUCE
3 tbsp rice vinegar
2 tbsp soy sauce
1 tsp cornflour
3 tbsp chicken stock or water
2½ tbsp caster sugar

★ Cut the beef across the grain into thin slices, then stack a few slices on top of each other and cut into slivers the size of long matchsticks. Whisk the eggs with the cornflour and a pinch of salt to make a batter. Add the meat. Stir well to coat. Slice the carrot and courgettes and cut them into matchsticks.

★ Mix the vinegar and soy sauce in a small bowl. In another bowl, stir together the cornflour and stock or water.

★ Fill a large wok a quarter full of oil and when the oil is just beginning to smoke, add the carrot and courgette and stir-fry for 1 minute. Remove and transfer to a dish lined with paper towels.

★ Reheat the oil and when starting to smoke add half the beef, using tongs to make sure the strips of beef remain separate. Fry until crispy, about 3–5 minutes, then drain and add to the carrot and courgettes. Repeat with the remaining beef.

★ Clean out the wok, add 1 tablespoon of oil, and when hot add the spring onions, chilli and garlic. Stir-fry for a few seconds, then add the cooked noodles.

★ Make the sauce by mixing the rice vinegar and soy sauce with the cornflour and stock and add the caster sugar. Add to the noodles, then toss with the beef and cooked vegetables. Stir-fry briefly until heated through.

Bow-tie Bolognese with cherry tomatoes

You could make this with or without the cheeses or just sprinkle with a mix of grated Parmesan and Cheddar and cook under a preheated grill until golden.

250 g (9 oz) bow-tie pasta
1 tbsp olive oil
1 red onion, finely chopped
1 red pepper, diced
2 garlic cloves, crushed
350 g (12 oz) lean minced beef
½ tsp balsamic vinegar
2 x 400 g (14 oz) tins cherry tomatoes
2 tbsp sun-dried tomato purée
1 tbsp ketchup
1 bay leaf
2 tsp brown sugar
3 tbsp basil, chopped
250 g (9 oz) mozzarella cheese, cubed
4 tbsp grated Parmesan

★ Cook the pasta according to the instructions on the packet. Drain.

★ Heat the oil in a saucepan and sauté the onion and red pepper for 5 minutes. Add the garlic and sauté for 1 minute. Add the mince and sauté, stirring occasionally, until browned. Add the balsamic vinegar and cook for 1 minute until evaporated. Add the cherry tomatoes, sun-dried tomato purée, ketchup, bay leaf and sugar. Bring up to the boil, then simmer for 25 minutes.

★ Add the cooked pasta to the pan with the basil and mix together. Transfer to a heatproof dish and scatter over the mozzarella and Parmesan before serving.

Spicy sausage meatball pasta

You can use any sausage you like but this recipe works well with spicy ones. There is a huge variety of different flavours in your supermarket. I used ones that have paprika in them, as this adds a smoky flavour to the sauce.

4 fat spicy sausages (Spanish or Italian sausages are best)
2 tbsp olive oil
1 large onion, finely chopped
2 garlic cloves, crushed
300 ml (10 fl oz) passata
150 ml (5 fl oz) vegetable or chicken stock
1 tsp sun-dried tomato purée
½ tsp sugar
½ tsp dried thyme or 1½ tsp fresh thyme
225 g (8 oz) fusilli pasta
grated Parmesan or Cheddar, to serve

★ Squeeze the sausage meat from their skins into a bowl and shape the meat into 16–20 small balls. Heat 1 tablespoon of oil in a small frying pan. Fry the meatballs until lightly golden but still raw in the middle.

★ Heat the remaining oil in a saucepan. Add the onion and garlic and sauté for 4 minutes. Add the remaining sauce ingredients and bring to the boil. Add the meatballs, cover with a lid, then gently simmer for 10 minutes.

★ Meanwhile, cook the pasta according to the instructions on the packet. Drain and add to the sauce.

★ Serve with some grated Parmesan or Cheddar sprinkled on top.

Bow-tie pasta with bacon and peas

Simple, cheap and tasty. A good dish to make when the cupboard is bare.

200 g (7 oz) bow-tie pasta
150 g (5½ oz) frozen peas
100 g (3½ oz) smoked bacon lardons
1 onion, finely chopped
50 ml (2 fl oz) boiling water
50 g (2 oz) Parmesan cheese, grated
2 tbsp parsley, chopped
salt and freshly ground black pepper

★ Cook the pasta in boiling salted water according to the instructions on the packet and add the peas 3 minutes before the end of the cooking time. Drain and set aside.

★ Fry the bacon lardons in a frying pan for 2 minutes. Add the onion and cook for another 5 minutes. Add the water and Parmesan, bring up to the boil, then add the pasta, peas and parsley. Season to taste.

FAVOURITE

FISH

Creamy cod with penne and prawns

Cod used to be really cheap but now, because of overfishing, it has become more expensive and if you buy it it should carry the MSC label for sustainability. I hope we never run out of it for fish and chips! There are other white fish you could use for this recipe, though. Hake is good and you could also use haddock. If you like, you could also add some peas about 3 minutes before the end of the cooking time.

250 g (9 oz) penne pasta
a knob of butter
2 large shallots, finely chopped
12 tbsp white wine vinegar
150 ml (¼ pint) fish stock
1 tbsp cornflour
200 ml (7 fl oz) full-fat crème fraîche
200 g (7 oz) cod fillet, skinned and sliced into 2-cm cubes
150 g (5½ oz) small cooked prawns
2 tbsp dill, chopped
1 large plum tomato, deseeded and chopped
50 g (2 oz) Parmesan, grated
salt and freshly ground black pepper

★ Cook the pasta in boiling salted water according to the packet instructions. Drain.

★ While the pasta is cooking, melt the butter in a saucepan. Add the shallots and sweat them for 2 to 3 minutes. Add the vinegar and stock, bring to the boil and reduce by half. Mix the cornflour with 2 tablespoons of cold water in a small bowl. Add to the stock and stir until thickened. Add the crème fraîche and bring back to the boil.

★ Add the cod, reduce the heat and simmer gently for 4 minutes. Add the prawns, dill and tomato, toss together with the pasta and Parmesan. Season and serve at once.

Salmon, prawn and dill lasagne

Ideally we should eat oily fish like salmon twice a week. Its good for the heart and good for the brain so it's good to find new ways to serve it, such as this tasty lasagne.

50 g (2 oz) butter
1 leek, finely chopped
1½ tsp white wine vinegar
50 g (2 oz) plain flour
600 ml (1 pint) milk
2 tbsp lemon juice
100 g (3½ oz) baby spinach
2 tbsp dill, chopped
50 g (2 oz) Parmesan cheese, grated
salt and freshly ground black pepper
300 g (10½ oz) salmon fillet,
    skinned and cut into 2-cm cubes
225 g (8 oz) cooked king prawns
150 g (5½ oz) broccoli, sliced into
    small florets and blanched
4 sheets lasagne
30 g (1 oz) Parmesan, grated

★ Preheat the oven to 200˚C/400˚F/Gas 6.

★ Melt the butter in a deep saucepan. Add the leek and gently sauté for 5 to 6 minutes until soft. Add the vinegar, then stir in the flour and cook over the heat until blended. Add the milk, bring to the boil, then stir until thickened. Add the lemon juice, spinach, dill and 50 g (2 oz) Parmesan. Stir over the heat until the spinach has wilted. Season with salt and black pepper.

★ Put a third of the salmon, prawns and broccoli into the base of a small ovenproof dish (about 21 x 16 x 7cm). Pour over a third of the sauce. Place two sheets of lasagne on top. Repeat with more of the fish mixture, sauce and the remaining lasagne sheets, then finish with a layer of the fish mixture and sauce.

★ Sprinkle with the 30 g (1 oz) Parmesan, then place in the oven for 30 minutes. Leave to stand for 5 minutes before serving.

Creamy cod with baby shell pasta

The wine reduction adds flavour to this dish – but don't worry, all the alcohol evaporates away. If you are using a stock cube, make sure you dilute it with the right amount of water, otherwise this could taste very salty.

1 small onion, finely diced
150 ml (¼ pint) white wine
200 ml (7 fl oz) fish stock
100 ml (3½ fl oz) double cream
½ tsp caster sugar
½ tsp lemon juice
2 tsp cornflour
1 tsp rice wine vinegar
300 g (10½ oz) cod fillet, skinned
   and cut into large pieces
2 tbsp chives, chopped
100 g (3½ oz) baby shell pasta
2 carrots, finely diced
100 g (3½ oz) frozen peas

★ Put the onion and white wine into a saucepan. Bring up to the boil, then reduce by two-thirds. Add the stock and reduce again by two-thirds. Add the double cream, sugar and lemon juice. Mix the cornflour with 1 tablespoon of cold water, then add it to the hot sauce and stir until thickened.

★ Add the vinegar to the pan, then the cod, and gently simmer for 4–5 minutes until just cooked. Add the chives and gently mix together.

★ Cook the pasta in boiling salted water for 8–10 minutes or according to the packet instructions. Add the carrots and peas 4 minutes before the end of the cooking time. Drain, spoon a little pasta onto a plate and spoon over the cod and the sauce.

Crab linguine

You can buy fresh crabmeat in the supermarket, and by mixing it with sautéed onion, garlic and chilli you can whip up a great pasta dish in minutes.

160 g (5½ oz) linguine
2 tbsp sunflower oil
40 g (1½ oz) white onions, peeled
   and chopped
40 g (1½ oz) red onions, peeled
   and chopped
1 garlic clove, crushed
6 g red chilli, finely chopped
170 g (6 oz) flaked fresh crabmeat
2 tbsp snipped chives
salt and freshly ground black pepper
   (preferably Cornish sea salt)
1 tbsp light olive oil

★ Cook the linguine according to the instructions on the packet. Drain.

★ Heat the sunflower oil in a large pan and sauté the onions, garlic and chilli for 3 minutes. Add the crabmeat and cook for 2 minutes.

★ Remove from the heat and stir in the snipped chives. Season with a little freshly ground black pepper and a little salt. Toss with the drained pasta and serve drizzled with the olive oil.

Teriyaki salmon with soba noodles and spring onions

Soba noodles are thin Japanese noodles made of buckwheat flour and in Japan it is traditionally considered polite to slurp noodles noisily. This would be fun to serve with child-friendly chopsticks. Mirin is a sweet Japanese rice wine which I use a lot in both salads and marinades.

250 g (9 oz) salmon fillet
2 tbsp teriyaki sauce
1 tsp mirin
1 tsp sake
160 g (5½ oz) soba noodles
60 g (2½ oz) spring onions, sliced
salt and freshly ground black
    pepper

★ Cut the salmon into large cubes. Mix together the teriyaki sauce, mirin and sake and pour over the salmon. Leave to marinate for 20 minutes.

★ Meanwhile, soak 4 bamboo skewers in water so that they don't burn when cooked, and cook the soba noodles in a pan of boiling salted water according to the packet instructions.

★ Preheat the oven to 220°C/425°F/Gas 7. Thread the salmon cubes onto the bamboo skewers. Bake the salmon skewers in the oven for 8 minutes.

★ Fold the spring onions through the noodles and season to taste. Place the salmon skewers on top of the noodles and serve.

VARIATION: Sauté the spring onion with a handful of beansprouts, stir in 1 tablespoon of teriyaki sauce and toss with the cooked noodles.

Spaghetti and mussels in a parcel

Shop around when buying mussels and select ones with tightly closed shells, avoiding any that are broken. It is best to eat mussels on the same day that you buy them. To clean them, place the mussels in a sink full of cold water and discard any that are open. Pull away the beards (see page 117) and give the shells a good scrub. Rinse a few times to make sure they are free of sand. Mussels need very little cooking – as soon as the shells are wide open they are cooked. Cooking them in a parcel seals in all the delicious flavours.

200 g (7 oz) spaghetti
½ red chilli, finely diced
3 garlic cloves, crushed
3 tbsp parsley, chopped
2 tbsp basil, chopped
3 tbsp olive oil
6 tbsp white wine
juice of ½ lemon
100 ml (3½ fl oz) fish stock
1 tsp sugar
salt and freshly ground black
    pepper
450 g (1 lb) live mussels, cleaned
grated Parmesan cheese, to
    serve (optional)

★ Preheat the oven to 200°C/400°F/Gas 6.
★ Cook the spaghetti in boiling salted water until just cooked. Drain and refresh in cold water.
★ Mix the remaining ingredients except the mussels in a large bowl. Add the cold spaghetti, season, and toss together.
★ Divide the pasta between 4 pieces of square tin foil that each measures 30 x 30cm. Divide the mussels between the parcels and spoon over any sauce that is left in the bowl. Season to taste. Fold in the edges and seal so that each parcel looks like a Cornish pasty.
★ Make a small hole in the top of each parcel, place them on a baking sheet and bake for 12–15 minutes until hot and the mussels have opened. Open the parcel and serve with a little Parmesan cheese, if you wish.

- MAKES 4 PORTIONS
- PREPARATION TIME: 18 MINUTES
- COOKING TIME: 25 MINUTES
- NOT SUITABLE FOR FREEZING

Marina's spaghetti with seafood

Seafood with spaghetti is one of my favourite meals. If you have some Noilly Prat this adds a great flavour to the dish. If you have never cooked seafood before don't worry: it's really very easy and the good news is it takes only minutes.

500 g (½ kg) mussels
250 g (9 oz) clams
2 tbsp olive oil
1 red onion, sliced
1 garlic clove, crushed
50 ml (2 fl oz) Noilly Prat
   or white wine (optional)
1 x 400 g (14 oz) can chopped
   tomatoes
100 ml (3½ fl oz) fish stock
Tabasco sauce
1 tsp sugar
salt and freshly ground
   black pepper
200 g (7 oz) spaghetti
250 g (9 oz) large fresh prawns,
   peeled, head removed and
   deveined
1 tbsp chopped fresh basil
1 tbsp lemon juice

★ Discard any mussels or clams that do not stay closed when gently pressed. Place the mussels and clams in a bowl of salt water for 10 minutes to extract any sand caught in the shells. If the mussel or clam shells still feel gritty after the initial soaking, scrub them under a cold running tap using a stiff brush. If the mussel or clam shells do not feel gritty after the initial soaking, they don't need to be scrubbed.

★ Use a damp kitchen towel and wipe the shells clean. Remove the beards from the mussels – these are the little fibrous tufts – by cutting them away with a knife or a scissors (some cultivated mussels don't have beards). Place the clams and mussels in a colander and give them a final rinse before using them. If you are not using them straightaway, store them in the fridge.

★ Heat the olive oil in a large saucepan and fry the onion and garlic for 7 to 8 minutes until soft. Add the Noilly Prat or wine, if using, bring to the boil and reduce by half. Add the chopped tomatoes, stock, Tabasco, sugar and salt and black pepper and cook for 10 minutes.

★ Meanwhile, cook the spaghetti according to the packet instructions. Drain.

★ Add all the seafood and basil to the tomato sauce, stir well, cover with a lid and cook for 3–4 minutes. Then stir in the cooked spaghetti and lemon juice just before serving.

- MAKES 4 PORTIONS
- PREPARATION TIME: 6 MINUTES
- COOKING TIME: 10 MINUTES
- NOT SUITABLE FOR FREEZING

Sea bass with ginger and spring onion on a bed of noodles

Sea bass is a delicate fish and the combination of mirin – a sweet rice wine – soy sauce, rice wine vinegar, garlic and ginger gives it a delicious Japanese flavour. Serve on a bed of noodles with beansprouts and sugar snap peas for a special occasion. For adults you can add some chopped red chilli when sautéing the garlic and ginger.

2½ tbsp olive oil
salt and freshly ground black
    pepper
4 seabass fillets, skin on
    (approx. 350 g/12 oz)
2-cm piece of fresh ginger,
    peeled and thinly sliced
2 garlic cloves
150 g (5½ oz) sugar snap peas,
    sliced
100 g (3½ oz) beansprouts
bunch spring onions, finely sliced
100 g (3½ oz) egg noodles
4 tbsp mirin
4 tbsp soy sauce
1 tsp rice wine vinegar

★ Heat 1½ tablespoons of oil in a large frying pan. Season the fish and slash the skin. Fry the fillets for 3–4 minutes, skin-side down over a high heat, until crispy. Turn over and cook for 1 minute. Remove to a plate and keep warm.

★ Heat the remaining oil. Add the ginger and garlic and fry for 2 minutes. Add the sugar snap peas, beansprouts and half the spring onions and stir-fry for 3 minutes.

★ Cook the noodles in boiling salted water according to the packet instructions. Drain, then add to the pan with the beansprouts. Season, then mix together the mirin, soy sauce and vinegar. Pour half of the sauce over the noodles and heat the rest in a small pan. Spoon some noodles onto a plate and place 1 fish fillet on top. Pour over the warm sauce and sprinkle over the remaining spring onions. Serve straight away.

- MAKES 2 PORTIONS
- PREPARATION TIME: 10 MINUTES
- COOKING TIME: 6 MINUTES
- NOT SUITABLE FOR FREEZING

Crunchy squid with rigatoni

Kids tend to love deep-fried squid and if you have never cooked squid before, it is really easy and quick. Make sure the squid is fresh, so try and cook on the day you buy it and don't overcook or it can go rubbery. As a variation, instead of using turmeric try making this with smoked Spanish paprika.

110 g (4 oz) rigatoni
125 g (4½ oz) squid, cleaned, scored, tentacles removed and cut into rings
80 g (3 oz) plain flour
salt and freshly ground black pepper
1 tsp turmeric
3 tbsp sunflower oil
100 g (3½ oz) sugar snap peas, cut into thin strips

★ Cook the rigatoni in a pan of salted water according to the instructions on the packet. Drain.

★ Cut the squid into rings. Pour the flour onto a plate, season with salt and black pepper and mix in the turmeric. Coat the squid in the seasoned flour. Heat the oil in a wok. You will know it is hot enough when you drop a cube of bread in the hot oil and it becomes golden and crispy. Shake off any excess flour from the squid and sauté the squid for 2–3 minutes until crispy. Don't overcrowd the pan – you can cook this in batches.

★ Meanwhile, blanch the sugar snap peas in boiling salted water, add to the squid and stir-fry for a few seconds. Drain the pasta and mix with the crunchy squid and sugar snap peas.

YUMMY
VEGGIES

🥣 MAKES 4 PORTIONS

🕐 PREPARATION TIME: 8 MINUTES

◉ COOKING TIME: 8 MINUTES

❄ PESTO SAUCE SUITABLE FOR FREEZING

Spaghetti with pesto

Adding parsley to the mixture helps to give a good green colour. You could add a few chopped SunBlush tomatoes to the spaghetti, too, or sprinkle with some pine nuts.

225 g (8 oz) spaghetti

PESTO SAUCE
50 g (2 oz) pine nuts
50 g (2 oz) Parmesan cheese, grated,
**   plus extra for serving**
1–2 garlic cloves
small bunch of parsley leaves
small bunch of basil leaves and stalks
a pinch of sugar
100 ml (3½ fl oz) olive oil
1 tbsp water
salt and freshly ground black pepper

★ Toast the pine nuts in a frying pan until lightly golden. Remove from the pan and leave to cool.

★ Cook the spaghetti in a large pan of lightly salted boiling water according to the instructions on the packet.

★ Meanwhile, tip the Parmesan, garlic, parsley, basil, sugar and cooled pine nuts into a food processor and whiz until finely chopped. Slowly add the olive oil while the motor is running. Add the water and season. Spoon into a small bowl.

★ Drain the cooked pasta and put it back into the saucepan. Add 4–5 tablespoons of pesto and toss together.

★ Sprinkle with extra Parmesan before serving.
(You can freeze any leftover pesto sauce for up to 2 months.)

- MAKES 6 PORTIONS
- PREPARATION TIME: 8 MINUTES
- COOKING TIME: 45 MINUTES
- SUITABLE FOR FREEZING

Spinach, ricotta and tomato lasagne

9 sheets no pre-cook or fresh lasagne

TOMATO SAUCE
2 tbsp olive oil
1 large onion, peeled and chopped
1 garlic clove, crushed
1 tbsp balsamic vinegar
2 x 400 g (14 oz) cans chopped
   tomatoes
4 tbsp SunBlush tomatoes, chopped
2 tbsp tomato purée

SPINACH AND RICOTTA FILLING
1 tbsp olive oil
½ small onion
500 g (18 oz) fresh spinach, washed
   and tough stalks removed
250 g (9 oz) ricotta cheese
2 tbsp grated Parmesan
salt and freshly ground black pepper

CHEESE SAUCE
30 g (1 oz) butter
30 g (1 oz) plain flour
450 ml (15 fl oz) milk
75 g (3 oz) grated Gruyère cheese
salt and freshly ground black pepper

4 tbsp freshly grated Parmesan
   cheese

★ Preheat the oven to 180°C/350°F/Gas 4.

★ To make the tomato sauce, heat the oil in a pan and sauté the onion and garlic for 4 minutes. Add the balsamic vinegar and cook for about 30 seconds. Drain half the juice from the cans of chopped tomatoes and add the tomatoes, SunBlush tomatoes and tomato purée. Bring to the boil and simmer for 10 minutes.

★ Meanwhile, make the filling. Heat the oil in another pan and sauté the onion for 4 minutes until softened. Stir in the spinach and cook until wilted, then squeeze out the excess water. Mix with the ricotta cheese and 2 tablespoons of freshly grated Parmesan and chop for a few seconds in a food processor. Season with a little salt and pepper. Set aside.

★ For the cheese sauce, melt the butter, stir in the flour and cook for about 1 minute. Gradually stir in the milk and cook for about 2 minutes until thickened. Stir in the grated Gruyère until melted and season to taste.

★ If using fresh lasagne, cook it in boiling lightly salted water first, according to the instructions on the packet.

★ To assemble the lasagne, spoon a third of the tomato sauce on the base of a fairly deep ovenproof dish (about 24 x 19 x 7cm) and cover with a layer of the spinach and ricotta mixture. Cover with 3 sheets of lasagne followed by a layer of tomato sauce. Repeat with each layer twice, finishing off with a layer of the cheese sauce.

★ Sprinkle over the remaining Parmesan cheese and bake in the oven for 30 minutes.

MAKES 4 PORTIONS

PREPARATION TIME: 15 MINUTES

COOKING TIME: 15 MINUTES

NOT SUITABLE FOR FREEZING

MAKES 6 PORTIONS

PREPARATION TIME: 8 MINUTES

COOKING TIME: 45 MINUTES

NOT SUITABLE FOR FREEZING

Vegetable fusilli

200 g (7 oz) fusilli pasta
50 g (2 oz) frozen peas
1 tbsp olive oil
1 large onion, finely chopped
1 garlic clove, crushed
1 small yellow pepper, cut into strips
100 g (4 oz) small broccoli florets
1 medium courgette
125 ml (4½ fl oz) crème fraîche
125 ml (4½ fl oz) vegetable stock
75 g (2½ oz) Parmesan, grated, plus
    extra to serve (optional)
6–8 medium-ripe tomatoes,
    skinned, deseeded and chopped
salt and freshly ground black pepper

★ Cook the pasta in a large pan of lightly salted boiling water according to the instructions on the packet and add the peas 4 minutes before the end of the cooking time. Drain the pasta and peas.

★ Heat the olive oil in a heavy-bottomed saucepan and sauté the onion and garlic for 1 minute. Add the yellow pepper, broccoli and courgette and sauté for about 8 minutes or until just tender. Stir in the crème fraîche and the vegetable stock. Bring up to the boil and reduce by a third. Add the Parmesan and season. Then add the tomatoes and simmer for 1 minute.

★ Add the drained pasta, courgette and peas and toss together. Serve with extra Parmesan to sprinkle on top if you wish.

Grandma's noodle pudding

225 g (8 oz) vermicelli or fine egg noodles
1 large egg , beaten
25 g (1 oz) butter, melted, plus a knob
    for the topping
100 ml (3½ fl oz) milk
2 tbsp vanilla sugar or 2 tbsp caster
    sugar and 1 tsp vanilla essence
½ tsp mixed spice
100 g (3½ oz) each sultanas and raisins
15 g (½ oz) flaked almonds (optional)

★ Preheat the oven to 180°C/350°F/Gas 4.

★ Cook the vermicelli or fine egg noodles in boiling salted water for about 5 minutes. Drain. Mix with the remaining ingredients, apart from the knob of butter.

★ Tip the mixture into a greased, shallow, ovenproof baking dish approximately 25 x 20cm. Dot with butter and bake for 40 minutes.

MAKES 2 PORTIONS

PREPARATION TIME: 6 MINUTES

COOKING TIME: 10 MINUTES

NOT SUITABLE FOR FREEZING

MAKES 6 PORTIONS

PREPARATION TIME: 10 MINUTES

COOKING TIME: 40 MINUTES

SUITABLE FOR FREEZING

Field, flat and wild mushroom tagliatelle

160 g (5½ oz) tagliatelle pasta
60 g (2½ oz) chestnut mushrooms
80 g (3 oz) flat or Portabello mushrooms
50 g (2 oz) wild or shitake mushrooms
1 tbsp sunflower oil
1 onion, diced
1 garlic clove, chopped
100 ml (3½ fl oz) crème fraîche
2 tsp chopped chives

★ Cook the tagliatelle in boiling salted water according to the instructions on the packet. Drain.
★ Slice all the mushrooms. Heat the oil and sauté the onion, garlic and mushrooms for 5 minutes. Add the crème fraîche and simmer. Fold in the chopped chives and season to taste.
★ Serve the drained tagliatelle with the sauce poured over.

Lentil soup with pasta

2 tbsp olive oil
1 large leek, roughly chopped
1 large celery stick, roughly chopped
1 large carrot, finely diced
100 g (3½ oz) dried red lentils
2 garlic cloves, crushed
1 x 400 g (14 oz) can chopped tomatoes
1.5 litres (2½ pints) chicken stock
2 tbsp sundried tomato purée
50 g (2 oz) small pasta shells
2 tbsp thyme, chopped
1 tbsp parsley, chopped
salt and freshly ground black pepper

★ Heat the oil in a deep saucepan. Add the leek, celery and carrot and sauté for 5 minutes. Add the lentils, garlic, tomatoes, chicken stock and sundried tomato purée. Bring up to the boil and simmer for 25 minutes until the lentils are just cooked.
★ Add the pasta and continue to simmer for 8–9 minutes until the pasta is cooked. Add the herbs and season to taste.

☺ MAKES 4 PORTIONS

🕐 PREPARATION TIME: 1 HOUR

☉ COOKING TIME: 5 MINUTES

❊ SUITABLE FOR FREEZING

Spinach and ricotta ravioli

PASTA
300 g (10½ oz) double zero
    'oo' flour, plus extra for dusting
3 large eggs
1 tsp salt
1 tbsp olive oil

FILLING
250 g (9 oz) baby spinach
100 g (4 oz) ricotta cheese
50 g (2 oz) Parmesan cheese, grated
1 egg yolk
a pinch of nutmeg

SAUCE
3 tbsp olive oil
1 large garlic clove, crushed
5 large ripe tomatoes, skinned,
    deseeded and roughly chopped

★ First make the pasta. Measure the flour, eggs, salt and oil into a bowl. Mix together with a wooden spoon, then knead it in the bowl, using your hands, to form a dough. Tip out onto a floured work surface and knead for 10 minutes until shiny and smooth. Wrap in cling film and rest for 10 minutes at room temperature.

★ Divide the dough into 4 balls. Roll out one ball to a small rectangle, then feed it through a pasta machine, starting on the widest setting. Go through each setting 2–3 times, working up from 1 to 5. Sprinkle flour over the sheets occasionally so they don't stick.

★ Cut the long sheet of pasta in half so you have 2 sheets that measure about 30 x 10 cm (12 x 4 in). Repeat with the remaining balls until you have 8 sheets. Leave to rest for 10 minutes.

★ Toss in flour, then place on a baking sheet dusted with flour. Cover with cling film. Alternatively, hang the pasta from a pasta stand.

★ To make the filling, wilt the spinach in a frying pan. Tip into a bowl and leave to cool, then add the remaining ingredients. Put one sheet of pasta on the work surface and spoon 6 teaspoons of the filling along the sheet. Brush a little water around the filling, put another sheet on top and press down around it to seal the edges. Cut around the fillings to make 6 squares, scoring the edges with a fork. Dust with flour and leave to dry for 30 minutes, turning halfway through. Repeat to make 24 squares.

★ To make the sauce, heat the oil in a saucepan. Add the garlic and tomatoes and warm through. Cook the ravioli in boiling salted water for 2–3 minutes. Drain, then serve with the sauce spooned over.

Butternut squash ravioli

FILLING
100 g (3½ oz) butternut squash
   (peeled weight)
40 g (1½ oz) ricotta
12 g (½ oz) Parmesan cheese,
   grated
½ tsp fresh sage
½ egg yolk
salt and freshly ground black
   pepper

TO SERVE
3 tbsp fresh green pesto sauce
   (see page 122)

★ To make the filling, steam the butternut squash in a steamer for 10–12 minutes until soft. Leave to cool. Mash the squash in a bowl using a fork. Add the remaining ingredients and season.
★ Make the ravioli as on page 128, making 24 squares.
★ Cook the ravioli in boiling salted water for 4 minutes. Drain, then gently toss in the pesto.

Three-cheese ravioli

FILLING
50 g (2 oz) ricotta cheese
50 g (2 oz) Parmesan, finely grated
50 g (2 oz) Gruyère cheese, finely
  grated
1 egg yolk
salt and freshly ground black pepper

TOMATO SAUCE
1 tbsp olive oil
1 onion, chopped
1 garlic clove, crushed
1 x 400 g (14 oz) can tomatoes
100 ml (3½ fl oz) water
1 tsp sundried tomato purée
dash of sugar

★ Mix all the filling ingredients together in a bowl and season well.
★ Make the ravioli as in the recipe on page 128.
★ To make the sauce, heat the oil in a saucepan, add the onion and garlic and sauté for 5 minutes. Add the tomatoes, water, sundried tomato purée and sugar. Cover and simmer for 15–20 minutes, then whiz with a hand blender until smooth.

- 🥣 MAKES 4 PORTIONS
- 🕐 PREPARATION TIME: 30 MINUTES
- 🕐 COOKING TIME: 1 HOUR 20 MINUTES
- ❄️ SUITABLE FOR FREEZING

Pumpkin gnocchi with butter and sage sauce

400 g (14 oz) Maris Piper potatoes
200 g (7 oz) sweet potatoes
300 g (10½ oz) pumpkin, cut into
    wedges, or ½ medium butternut
    squash, seeds and fibre removed
a knob of butter
100 g (3½ oz) plain flour, plus
    extra for dusting
1 egg yolk
1 litre (1¾ pints) vegetable stock

Butter and sage sauce:
2 tbsp sunflower oil
1 small onion, peeled and finely
    chopped
2 tbsp fresh sage leaves, finely
    sliced
110 g (4 oz) butter
finely grated zest of 1 lemon
salt and freshly ground black
    pepper

★ Preheat the oven to 180°C/350°F/Gas 4.

★ Prick the potatoes and sweet potatoes all over using a fork. Place on a large baking sheet with the pumpkin wedges or the butternut squash, skin-side down. Melt the butter and use it to brush the flesh of the pumpkin or butternut squash. Bake the vegetables for 1 hour or until they are tender. Remove from the oven and allow to cool.

★ Cut the potatoes in half and scoop the flesh into a bowl, along with that of the pumpkin or butternut squash. Either put the vegetables through a mouli or mash thoroughly and put into a large bowl. Sift in the flour, add the egg yolk and mix with a wooden spoon. Season.

★ Fit a piping bag with a 2 cm (¾ in) nozzle and fill with some of the mixture. Pipe lengths of gnocchi onto a floured baking sheet, then cut into 2 cm (¾ in) pieces before poaching in a pan of boiling vegetable stock, or squeeze the mixture out of the the piping bag and cut into 3 cm (1 in) lengths so that the pieces drop straight into the boiling stock. Cook for about a minute, until they float to the surface. Remove them carefully with a slotted spoon and arrange them on a baking sheet. You will need to cook the gnocchi in about four batches.

★ To make the butter and sage sauce, heat the oil and sauté the onion for 3–4 minutes until softened but not coloured. Add the sage and sauté for 30 seconds. Stir in the butter until melted, then remove from the heat and stir in the lemon zest. Season to taste with salt and pepper. Serve the gnocchi with the melted sage butter drizzled on top.

MAKES 4 PORTIONS

PREPARATION TIME: 15 MINUTES

COOKING TIME: 30 MINUTES

NOT SUITABLE FOR FREEZING

Spaghetti with tomato, mozzarella and spinach

1 tbsp olive oil
150 g (5½ oz) baby spinach
salt and freshly ground black pepper
½ red onion, finely chopped
1 red chilli, finely diced
2 garlic cloves, crushed
1 x 400 g (14 oz) can whole plum
   tomatoes
1 tbsp brown sugar
1 tbsp tomato ketchup
1 tbsp tomato purée
250 g (9 oz) spaghetti
2 large fresh plum tomatoes,
   deseeded and roughly chopped
1 x 250 g (9 oz) ball mozzarella, cubed
2 tbsp basil, roughly chopped

★ Heat 1 teaspoon of the oil in a wok or deep frying pan. Sauté the spinach for 2–3 minutes until wilted. Season and set aside.

★ Heat the remaining oil in a wok and sauté the onion for 6–8 minutes. Add the chilli and garlic and fry for 1–2 minutes. Add the canned tomatoes, sugar, ketchup and purée, then reduce the sauce over a medium heat for 10–12 minutes until thickened.

★ Cook the spaghetti in boiling salted water according to the instructions on the packet.

★ Add the fresh tomatoes to the tomato sauce with the spinach and cook for 3–4 minutes.

★ Add the drained pasta. Toss together and season well. Add the mozzarella and basil and serve.

- MAKES 6 PORTIONS
- PREPARATION TIME: 30 MINUTES
- COOKING TIME: 50 MINUTES
- SUITABLE FOR FREEZING

Mushroom and ricotta cheese cannelloni with pesto

**MUSHROOM AND
RICOTTA CHEESE FILLING**
1 tbsp olive oil
1 onion, finely chopped
1 garlic clove, crushed
250 g (9 oz) chestnut mushrooms, chopped
250 g (9 oz) ricotta cheese
1 egg yolk
85 g (3 oz) Parmesan cheese, grated
salt and freshly ground black pepper
12 cannelloni tubes

TOMATO SAUCE
1 x 400 g (14 oz) can chopped tomatoes
2 tbsp sun-dried tomato paste
2 tbsp fresh thyme leaves, chopped

PESTO SAUCE
50 g (2 oz) butter
50 g (2 oz) flour
600 ml (1 pint) milk
3 tbsp pesto
100 g (3½ oz) Parmesan cheese

★ Preheat the oven to 180°C/350°F/Gas 4.
★ First make the filling. Heat the oil in a saucepan and cook the onion for 5–6 minutes until soft. Add the garlic and mushrooms and continue to fry for another 5 minutes until the mushrooms are cooked and the pan is dry. Tip into a bowl and leave to cool. When cool, add the ricotta, egg yolk and Parmesan and season. Using your hands or a spoon, stuff the cannelloni tubes with the mixture.
★ Make the tomato sauce by simply mixing together all the ingredients in a bowl.
★ Finally, make the pesto sauce. Melt the butter in a saucepan. Add the flour and stir over the heat for 1 minute. Add the milk slowly, stirring until blended. Bring up to the boil and simmer for 2 minutes. Season, and add the pesto and 50 g (2 oz) of Parmesan.
★ Spoon the tomato sauce into the base of an ovenproof dish. Place the filled cannelloni tubes on top in a single layer. Pour over the pesto sauce so they are completely covered. Sprinkle the remaining cheese on top. Bake for 40 minutes until golden brown and soft.

⊌ MAKES 6 PORTIONS

◔ PREPARATION TIME: 1 HOUR

◔ COOKING TIME: 12 MINUTES

❄ SUITABLE FOR FREEZING

Fresh spinach tagliatelle

PASTA
100 g (3½ oz) baby spinach
300 g (10½ oz) double zero
  'oo' flour, plus extra for dusting
2 eggs
1 egg yolk
1 tbsp olive oil
1 tsp salt

50–75 g (2–3 oz) unsalted butter
50 g (2 oz) Parmesan, finely grated
salt and freshly ground black
  pepper

★ First make the pasta. Measure the spinach into a frying pan with 1 tablespoon of water. Fry over a high heat until wilted. Drain and squeeze out most of the liquid, roughly chop and leave to cool. Put the remaining ingredients into a bowl with the spinach. Mix with a wooden spoon, then knead with your hands to form a dough. Knead on a floured work surface for 10 minutes until shiny and smooth. Wrap in cling film and rest for 30 minutes at room temperature.

★ Divide the dough into 4 balls. Roll out to a small rectangle using a rolling pin. Feed through a pasta machine, starting with the widest setting. You will need to go through each setting 2–3 times working up from 1 to 5. Sprinkle with flour occasionally. Repeat with the remaining pasta until you have 4 long sheets.

★ Divide each sheet into 2, so you have 8 sheets in total. Hang the sheets on a pasta stand with wooden posts to rest for 10 minutes. Carefully feed the sheets through the tagliatelle cutter on the pasta machine. Toss in a little flour, then place on a baking sheet dusted with a little flour. Cover with cling film until needed.

★ Bring a pan of boiling salted water to the boil. Add the pasta and boil for 1½–2 minutes. Drain. Add the butter to the hot saucepan and gently melt. Add the pasta, salt and pepper and half of the Parmesan. Toss together and serve with the remaining cheese scattered on top.

TIP: You can make dough in a free-standing mixer such as a Kitchen Aid using a dough hook. Measure all the ingredients into the bowl and whiz until it has formed a ball. Tip out and knead for 10 minutes.

MAKES 4–5 PORTIONS

PREPARATION TIME: 25 MINUTES

COOKING TIME: 1 HOUR

SUITABLE FOR FREEZING

Vegetarian pasta bake with a crunchy topping

1 tbsp olive oil

1 medium aubergine, sliced into 2-cm cubes

1 red pepper, cut into 1 cm cubes

1 large courgette, cut into 1-cm cubes

1 red onion, sliced into wedges

10 g (½ oz) chestnut mushrooms, thinly sliced

2 garlic cloves, crushed

½ red chilli, finely diced

1 x 400 g (14 oz) can chopped tomatoes

300 ml (½ pint) vegetable stock

1 tbsp sundried tomato purée

50 g (2 oz) mature Cheddar cheese, grated

1 x 250 g (9 oz) ball vegetarian mozzarella, cut into cubes

6 sheets lasagne

50 g (2 oz) fresh breadcrumbs

50 g (2 oz) sunflower seeds

★ Preheat the oven to 200°C/400°F/Gas 6.

★ Heat the oil in a deep frying pan, add the aubergine and fry over a high heat for 4–5 minutes until lightly golden. Add the remaining vegetables, garlic and chilli and sauté for another 5 minutes. Add the tomatoes, stock and sundried tomato purée. Bring to the boil, cover with a lid and simmer for 20–25 minutes until the vegetables are soft and the liquid has thickened.

★ Divide the mixture into four. Put one quarter into the base of an ovenproof dish. Sprinkle a little Cheddar and mozzarella over the top. Place two sheets of lasagne on top. Repeat so you have three layers of pasta and four layers of tomato and vegetable sauce. Sprinkle over the breadcrumbs on the last layer of sauce, then top with the sunflower seeds.

★ Bake for 25–30 minutes until golden on top and the pasta is cooked in the middle.

MAKES 3 PORTIONS

PREP TIME: 8 MINUTES (PLUS MARINATING)

COOKING TIME: 8 MINUTES

NOT SUITABLE FOR FREEZING

MAKES 2 PORTIONS

PREPARATION TIME: 6 MINUTES

COOKING TIME: 24 MINUTES

SAUCE SUITABLE FOR FREEZING

Spaghettini with tomato salsa

TOMATO AND BASIL SALSA
6 large ripe tomatoes, deseeded
    and roughly chopped
¼–½ red chilli, deseeded and
    finely chopped
½ red onion, finely diced
1 small garlic clove, crushed
50 g (2 oz) SunBlush tomatoes,
    chopped, plus 3 tbsp oil from the jar
small bunch of basil, roughly chopped
2 tbsp white wine vinegar
salt and freshly ground black pepper
200 g (7 oz) spaghettini
freshly grated Parmesan, to serve

★ Measure all the salsa ingredients into a large bowl, season with salt and pepper and set aside to marinate for 1 hour out of the fridge.
★ Cook the spaghettini in boiling salted water according to the instructions on the packet. Drain, then add to the salsa ingredients. Toss together in the bowl until coated and serve with some freshly grated Parmesan.

Easy tomato sauce

1 ½ tbsp sunflower oil
1 onion, chopped
1 garlic clove, crushed
400g tin chopped tomatoes
1 tbsp tomato purée
1 tbsp sundried tomato purée
1 tsp sugar
150 g (5 oz) spaghetti or fusilli
2 tbsp fresh basil leaves
salt and freshly ground black pepper

★ Heat the oil in a pan. Add the onion and garlic and sauté for 4 minutes. Add the tomatoes, tomato purées and sugar. Bring to the boil, cover and simmer for 20 minutes.
★ Meanwhile, cook the pasta according to the packet instructions. Drain.
★ Tear the basil into pieces and stir into the tomato sauce. Season with salt and black pepper and toss the pasta with the tomato sauce.

index

Annabel Karmel is the UK's best-selling author on baby and children's food and nutrition. She is an expert in devising tasty and nutritious meals for children without the need for parents to spend hours in the kitchen.

A mother of three, Annabel is the number-one parenting author in the UK and fourth best-selling cookery writer. She has written 19 books on feeding babies and children (as well as teaching children how to cook), including *Complete Family Meal Planner*, *The Fussy Eaters Recipe Book* and the *Princess Party Cookbook*. Her books have sold over 4 million copies worldwide. Her *Complete Baby and Toddler Meal Planner* has become the authoritative guide on feeding babies and children and is regularly in the top five cookery titles.

Books are not the only string to Annabel's bow; she has created the Eat Fussy range of chilled meals, which is now the number-one range of branded ready meals for children in supermarkets. She has the popular Make it Easy range of equipment for preparing baby food. Annabel has also created a co-branded range of Healthy Foods for young children with Disney, and has developed her own collection of cooking equipment for aspiring junior chefs.

Annabel is passionate about improving the way children eat in popular family attractions, hotels, pubs and restaurants, and her menus can be found in all the major theme parks including Legoland and Thorpe Park, as well the UK's largest Holiday Park group – Haven Holidays and Butlins. In 2009 Annabel won a prestigious Caterer and Hotelkeeper Excellence in Food award for her children's meals, as well as the Lifetime Achievement award at the Mother and Baby Awards in 2009.

Her popular website www.annabelkarmel.com has more than 80,000 members, and offers parents delicious recipes for babies, children and adults, as well as information on all aspects of nutrition.

Annabel writes regularly for national newspapers and magazines and also appears frequently on radio and television as the expert on child nutritional issues, including *This Morning*, *BBC Breakfast*, Sky News and Radio 2, 4 and 5 amongst others. She was recently voted as one of the iconic chefs of her generation for ITV's *This Morning*.

Annabel was awarded an MBE in June 2006 in the Queen's Birthday Honours for her outstanding work in the field of child nutrition.

www.annabelkarmel.com

acknowledgements

My children, Nicholas, Lara and Scarlett who have eaten their way through this book. Lucinda Kaizik, Marina Magpoc and Leee Maycock for fun times in the kitchen assisting me in testing recipes. Seiko Hatfield, my wonderful food stylist. Dave King for his stunning photography and Jo Harris for the props. Mary Jones my publicist. My mother Evelyn Etkind for her endless support. Aurelia Stearns, my beautiful cover model. Everyone at Ebury, including Carey Smith, Fiona Macintyre, Sarah Lavelle, Louise McKee, Sarah Bennie and Helena Caldon. All at Smith & Gilmour. All the gorgeous models: Lily and Oscar Smith, Carina Skalicky, Storm Chambers and Madelaine Hamilton.

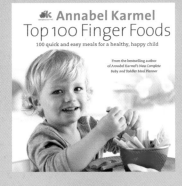

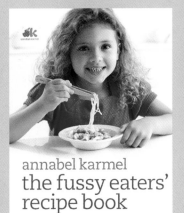

Making it fresh…for less

Making your own baby food could not be easier with my **Make It Easy** range of food preparation equipment that helps you to mash, steam, store and freeze fresh homemade food for your baby and toddler. Convenient, economical and easy to use when at home or out for the day.

In this range, there are also three organic baby pasta – **Baby Shell Pasta, Alphabet Pasta** and the innovative **Gluten Free Pasta Stars** – all ideal to use with my recipes found in this book.

For busy mums and fussy kids!

One of seven delicious toddler meals from my **Eat Fussy** range. This Bolognese Pasta Bake is made with a delicious tomato and hidden vegetable sauce topped with Cheddar cheese that will tempt the fussiest eater! A great meal solution when short of time, going out or simply pop in the freezer for later use! Also in the range: the bestselling **Salmon & Cod Fish Pie** and the comforting **Beef Cottage Pie**.

All ranges available from major retailers and supermarkets

Visit **www.annabelkarmel.com** for more delicious recipes, nutritional advice and a friendly forum for Mums. You can also be inspired by videos of Annabel cooking at **www.annabelkarmel.tv**

BROCCOLISPINACHO
ILMEATBALLSBUTTE
CHERRYTOMATOSGNO
PEPPERSPARSLEYPA
SPAGHETTINOODLEP
AWNSRAVIOLIMOZZA
LASAGNEPEASOLIVE
STOTAGLIATELLEFA
ACONMINESTRONESA
ETTEVEALEGGSBUTT
LCHIPOLATAROSEMA
CARPONEBREADCRUM
BALSAMICVINEGART